Futurology Express

Philip McShane

M.Sc., Lic. Phil., S.T.L., D.Phil. (Oxon.)

Axial Publishing

Vancouver

Printed in Canada by
Grandview Printing Co. Ltd.
Vancouver, Canada

Email: info@grandviewprinting.com

Axial Publishing

www.axialpublishing.com

Canadian Cataloguing in Publication Data

McShane, Philip 1932 -

Futurology Express

ISBN 978-0-9780945-5-3

1. Economics 2. Philosophy 3. Theology I. Title

Text layout and cover:
James Duffy
Christina Ghorayeb
Patrick Brown
Fátima Lizárraga Vega

To my wife, Reverend Sally,

"a ruddy gem of changeful light"

"A ruddy gem of changeful light"
Sir Walter Scott (1814)

"Standing naked to the world 120 feet above the sea outside on the balcony is a novel experience to say the least." Charles Riding, "A Quiet Night in the Bell Rock Lighthouse," 1998. Riding was one of the last keepers in the 1980s. The lighthouse was automated in 1988. It was built by a gallant group led by the engineer Robert Stevenson two hundred years ago, and visited by Sir Walter Scott in 1814.

Contents

Preface

The aim here is to give you a decent grasp of a new global hope. There are no references, no footnotes, at least not for the first fifteen chapters: this is just a chat that could lift your spirited molecules in the molasses of the present accumulation of global stupidities and horrors. The chat among the clinging horrors needs humor, and I'll throw in some, indeed immediately. There is a type of Irish saying that is comically contradictory, and one such occurs to me as I begin: "When you have your back to the wall, it's time to turn and run." Many think at present, be they politicians or poets, ecologists or nurses, that we have our backs to the wall. Then, says I, it's time to turn around. Turn around in what way? Well, that is the question that my little book is going to suggest an answer to in relatively plain words. Indeed, I am going to express futurology in a way that shows you the possibility of you riding, if not starting up or even driving, the express mentioned in the title.

My first chapter aims at hinting that this way has a decent probability, and that the rolling forward, after the tough job of the first push, will happen with growing ease. In a century or four, people will wonder why the express did not begin to roll in the nineteenth century, when the iron horse began tracking round the world. If that had happened, then perhaps we would not have stumbled and fumbled through world wars into groupings like the League of Nations, the United Nations, the World Bank, the International Monetary Fund, into the era of protesting and financial messing that serves our daily diet of bad news. Not to speak of reports of sick groupings of cartels and sexploiters, terrorists and lobbyists, etc., etc., etc. Indeed, the shift is to speak of groupings of a radically new type.[1]

---

[1] The groupings that I write of are quite beyond the dense searchings of Arjun Appadurai, *The Future as Cultural Fact: Essays on the Global Condition* (New York:

But what other groupings have I in mind? Those of a secular bent should be of good cheer with my offer: I am not going to invite you to turn to any of the various religious or semi-religious groupings, oriental or occidental or southern. I will have more to say about that later, in chapters 19 and 20. Rather, I am going to invite you to envisage new secular groupings that yet are so obvious and obviously needed that you may wonder, like the people of later centuries, about the slow start.

Enough of prefacing except to say that I do make up for skipping great names and elaborate footnotes starting with chapter 16. It had been my intention when I began to hold out on such references and notes till the Epilogue. But then, even earlier, it had been my intention to have just eight neat chapters. Let me, however, leave that topic of chapters and their content to the Epilogue.

You might like to go browsing now in the chapters after the fifteenth, to see from whom I stole the ideas, or you could visit www.philipmcshane.ca for a larger sniff of the context of my effort. But you would probably find the presentations there overly obscure and complex. Here, in the first fifteen chapters, I swing forward to express futurology in plain English, hoping that someone else Twitters it into more effective operation in some new e-line. If you Google futurology at present you'll find a common view that there is little future in futurology. I hope to persuade you, on the contrary, that it is to be a fully-effective science. By science, however, I mean something quite different from our present stale conventions. Dealing with that is part of the

---

Verso Press, 2013). But this book and his other writings add a rich context to our own brief searchings here. We also share an interest in the fate of India, being colonized at present by the pamperers of the West, and he provides a rich relevant context in Part 2 of his work. His title, of course, is catchy, even though the future is not a cultural fact. The future is massively threatened by consistent stupidity and cupidity. I refer to this book later simply as *The Future as Cultural Fact*.

turnaround of the futurology express. But certainly we could start with a web-reach.

My frontispiece must initially be a puzzle. I was led to it by my wife Sally, who has a way of fermenting images and references. In one bright moment of her searchings she revealed Robert Southey's title, "The Inchcape Rock," sending my Proustian reach back almost seventy years. What odd book or teacher led me there then? *The Inchcape Rock* is an earlier name for the Bell Rock on which Robert Stevenson built the lighthouse in 1807–11, a feat considered to be one of the wonders of the modern world. There is no difficulty in Googling it. Its story took my fancy, and obviously I associate it with the Tower of Able, an image of the collaborative dynamics about which I will say more later.

There is also the poem of Robert Southey telling the tale of the rock, and the putting of a bell on it to save lives. "The Abbot of Aberbrothok / Had placed that bell on the Inchcape Rock; / On a buoy in the storm it floated and swung, / And over the waves the warning rung." But there came later the pirate Sir Ralph the Rover: "Sir Ralph bent over from the boat, / And he cut the bell from the Inchcape float."

The story and its imaging caught my fancy. The monk Aquinas put a bell of logic on the rough-sea rocks of life. The rover of modernity has shaken it loose. Robert Stevenson planned the rotating red and white light that impressed Sir Walter Scott. Storm-tossed logic is replaced by a lightsome vortex of method that, marvelously, is to go with the flow and wit the flow. Of course, the image fails to capture the amazing global dynamics of the new omnidisciplinary Vorticism, and the shift from philosophy and theology to futurology. That is the story I wish you to tell yourself, with my rambling help.

Introduction

This is a strange book, but I wish to keep the topic of its strangeness and complexity and ambitions to the Epilogue: except for one ambition. My ambition is to involve you in making a radical and effective difference in the large domain of global progress. I wish you to share, in an effective manner, my optimism about what I call *Futurology*. I wish you not to be helpless, whether you are one of those who have occupied offensively some symbol of Wall Street's idiocy or have stood in some square clamoring for rights in a tyrannical regime or, perhaps worse, in a smiling tailored pseudo-democracy. Is Canada, where I live, such a democracy? It has a better reputation than most, but a recent little book presents our present leader, Stephen Harper, as *Fearmonger*.[2] Are we, in Canada, helpless in the face of his agenda? But the issue I raise here is the global possibility of shifting solidly and effectively from long-term helplessness to a massively new control of human meaning that will take the control of our globe away from the tyrants and touts and tricksters and gun-toters that are too evidently in charge. Another of the recent Canadian books on my desk is titled *The Resilience Imperative*.[3] It is full of bright and subtle suggestions but ends with a vague, ineffectual final chapter, "From Cultural Captivity to Focused Intention," and an Epilogue titled "The Great Transition," which give little hope of such a transition. Yet I would wish to steal those titles and wrap them round my own invitation to a shared "focused transition" that, yes, is to be effective. But, as I hope to intimate, it is to be a massively slow, patient transition. It would be quite silly to think otherwise. *The*

---

[2] Paula Mallea, *Fearmonger: Stephen Harper's Tough-on-Crime Agenda* (Toronto: James Lorimer, 2011).

[3] Michael Lewis and Pat Conaty, *The Resilience Imperative: Cooperative Transitions to a Steady-state Economy* (British Columbia, Canada: New Society Publishers, 2012).

Sorrows of Empire[4] will cripple us for the rest of this century, while China rises, Europe collapses, and Africa remains subtly colonized. My own native land is in an economic shambles and today, as I write, old taped phone calls of the greedy monsters behind the collapse have been finally made available. Allied Irish Banks' top men chat about dumping their mess on the Central bank. "How much is needed?" "Well, let's try 6 billion." "Where did you get that number?" "I pulled it out of my arse."

I mention banking and the shambles of economics because these are at the heart of the crisis. The meaning of both money and credit disappeared radically from global cultures in the middle of the last century. In that century, and the two centuries prior, there never was a serious economic science, a serious political economy, but in more recent times there has been an arrogant self-serving cover-up of its absence. The cover-up reached massive destructive heights in the past few decades, but in the past few months it has weakened as governors of banks and ministers of finance putter with printing money and stutter about the significance of their strategies. And meantime the money game goes on in the penthouses of the allied world bankers.

I might well have kept the focus of the book on the madness and malice that surrounds economics and its layers of politickings, but my ambition is larger, reaching for an omnidisciplinary collaborative transformation of global culture that is to shift from fantasy to fact in these next nine millennia. On that crazy note it seems best that I turn to a brief description of where we are going in this short chat.

It is a casual chat, and as I mentioned in the Preface, footnoting is avoided in my first fifteen chapters. I would wish you to ramble with me and do so in the paradox of being a sort-of detached

---

[4]Chalmers Johnson, *The Sorrows of Empire: Militarism, Secrecy, and the End of the Republic* (New York: Henry Holt, 2004).

interested reader yet still invited by me towards being your best self—and that effectively—and doing so even if you stay on the edge of my mad enterprise of establishing an effective science of the future, a globally-effective futurology.

I might well have written further here on the individual chapters, but that writing would give away, and all too vaguely indeed, the weaving that went into their structuring. That structuring emerged only slowly, starting with a quite simple plan, mentioned in the Preface, of a set of straightforward chapters. But once I broke from that plan the weaving began, and in chapter 16, as you will see, it took a further spontaneous twist.

I leave all that accounting for my twists and turns to the Epilogue. But the one turn that is to emerge immediately, if we are to get off the down-spiral of global folly, is the turn to ourselves. The futurology express depends on us getting our own little **whats** on track.

Chapter 1
The Turn-Around

When you have your back to the wall, turn around.

That was a twist on a piece of Irish humor mentioned in the Preface, a twist which we now follow up in a very elementary way.

First, you must note that the turn-around I write of is best illustrated by groups that are in trouble, not perhaps in major trouble, but at least in some sort of a rut of decay or staleness. The group with which I lead us on is a group that comes from memories of living in Toronto, Canada, where a simple conventional summer holiday consisted in your family heading north to some lakeshore rental cottage, or to an owned cottage if you had the family history of such a level of finance. You may already be with me in your memories, memories of childhood joys that somehow faded in teenage frustration. But let us start with my invented family and leave our own past out of it for the moment. As you well know, it is easier to solve the problems of the family or the person next door. We'll get back to that as we ramble along. Meantime, meet the Fewcares, an extended family of six people.

My story is of a Toronto family that has a holiday cottage at a lake some hundreds of kilometers north of the city. Follow your own images here, be they of escaping as a child from Mexico City or Moscow or Mumbai. I muddle the national names here, thinking first of Molly and Poldy Bloom. In the fourth year of their marriage they inherited a cottage from Molly's father, who had passed on. Molly's mother was living with them from then on. At that stage there were the two children, a year apart: Zack at 3 years of age, and Till, a year younger. Now the parents are in their early forties and the family holiday has been a matter of an extended family of six going to the cottage in July. The fifth member was, of course, Molly's mother with the odd nickname of Moses—a twist on her original Gaelic name. The sixth member of the group was a lonely brother of Poldy, Sean Tseng—did I mention that Poldy was Chinese?—who was much older than Poldy and lived alone. In those early days, Molly and Poldy did the decent thing and brought the bachelor family uncle with them on holidays: it was handy, anyway, to have a baby sitter for both Grandma Moses and the two young kids. It allowed Molly and Poldy freedom for occasional outings.

You have the scenario now, and can view it over the two decades. Zack and Till, who are unmarried at 23 and 22, are still living at home. Sean is now 55 and Grandma Moses is 72. By the way, you may find Sean and Poldy strange names for Chinese? I have a Chinese acquaintance named Sean. Often enough I find that my Asian immigrant friends pick some sound-equivalent of their own language-name. But my acquaintance's name pronounced in Chinese did not resemble at all the noise Shawn (that is, the Irish noise, e.g., my own name in Gaelic is pronounced Mockshawn). I asked him where he got the name Sean. He said that when he arrived in Canada he thought it was a great Canadian name! Poldy? Well, go figure. It does echo a Chinese name. But no matter: back to our group and its problems.

You may already have sensed the problems. Molly and Poldy are the central characters running the show. They see the happy extended family together on vacation as a great thing: the family who plays together stays together. And yes, those early years were wonderful: two small children splashing around in the lake in the presence of four loving adults. You can smile over a possible longer story, one that, depending on the talent of the author, could delve into the psychology of adults in their thirties and kids in their teens, even generate twistings and twitterings of dialogue within the layers of musics of the decades. But on we go with the story.

Changes in the life-styles of uncle and grandmother occur. Tseng is a settled alcoholic now, and prefers to stay a dollar's-throw away from the liquor store; grandma lives for Bingo at night with her downtown group. Not to speak of the surging sexuality of Zack and Till, reduced to phone sex and masturbatory joy by holiday isolation. Why, anyway, are they still at home at their ages? Have you not witnessed parallel settledness, even experienced it, globally or locally? I leave this to your musing now and to later chatting.

But obviously something has to give, and it "gives" or is given one particular spring when the question of July arrangements emerges. What gives?

Let us allow for luck: Till, at 22, is into management studies, with a focus on conflict management. When the spring conversation about holidays heats up, Till emerges as the voice of reason, the initial reason being: 'cool it clan, let's come up with a plan!' Zack, who has been reading Proust—in French of course, for his degree—calls for some memory-lane stuff, remembrance of times past, grandma's tea and cake, Tseng's violin melodies. Whatever.

So: they come up with a plan. But note now the turn-around. They come up with a plan about planning!

O.K., I admit that I am verging on the fantastic here: but is this not what expressing futurology is about?

Zack and Till prevail. The group is going to try some memory-lane work, and management studies suggest that they divide that work up. Here, again, I skim along: the entire book deals with just how the work can and should be divided. This story and its results were developed in lectures to young ladies in my teaching days in Nova Scotia and the process became communal fun: especially since many had suffered conventional family ways back home in Cape Breton, the north of the Province.

How to divide up the work, and what work? Our university classes even moved to envisage someone tackling remote factors like weather conditions and climate changes over the years as well as someone else sorting out the proximate and obvious settledness of the adults as compared to the bounce and jounce of youth. Timetables of events and habits of the group over the years had to be somehow catalogued. Somehow? The talents of the group came into play. Poldy was good at listing and dating events over years. Zack and Grandma were story-tellers.

The varying talents of my classes came into play also. Some got way ahead of others in thinking of past and present, or even the divisions of policy, planning, and action-decisions. Days of rambling and insight generated what seemed an obvious way to plan planning. Yes, you need lists done by whomever, but you need to sort out the meaning and use of those lists in the different years, and you need to somehow get the whole messy story together if you are to see your way forward. Here, amazingly, you can find the seeds of four functions that are the first half of our futurology express! The precocious ones had to be slowed down in their reach for policies.

Let Gran and Zack, perhaps, organize all past stuff for the two age groups, so that eventually we get to review the stories for what was good or bad about the holidays. We? Well, let's split the work again there. But we need to do it in some orderly fashion: otherwise we are into the bickering that Till is trying to steer us clear of.

After a few messy class days, we find that, yes, the group can come up with the basis of a fresh start on planning: what do each of us want, and where is each of us going, and where are we going together? Amazingly, the class agrees that this makes sense, that making sense is the key to the whole business, and from the demand to make sense we arrive at the final stages of settling on a holiday. We are finding our way to figuring out the second forward-looking phases of futurology. From our basic expression of wants there follows sets of general policies about a sane holiday. From policy there emerges a loose planning—looseness was seen as vital to sane togetherness—and then something we agreed to call executive reflection was required to really get the plan, literally, on this year's road by selecting relevant facets of the broader planning to fit this summer's particulars.

What sort of plans for the holiday turned up in the broader viewing? Indeed, there were all sorts of plans, some sound, some hilarious. We were reminded of George Burns' quip: "It's great to have a big happy family—in another town!" But what was amazing was that we came up with a very plausible structured plan for planning, where planning in its original sense was seventh in a structured list of eight jobs. Might you have a shot at sorting them out? But I leave that sorting out to chapter 4. Still, why not have a shot at mapping out the eight stages? You are to find that such a shot, properly brooded over, is the core of the transition to futurology.

The old guy in Toronto who originally put me onto this began by remarking how easy it was, and he gave his version of the strategy using his eight fingers, four related to the past doings, four relating to the future. But he also chuckled later over a story about Columbus who was listening to a group of grandees talking about the simplicity of discovering America. Columbus presented them with an egg, and presented them as well with the challenge of standing it on its end. The problem left them baffled. Columbus eventually took the egg from the baffled group and, dinging the blunt end, stood it on that end.

Much later the old guy in Toronto remarked that the new perspective was likely to be shunned, even laughed at, until someone slipped into the view that they had discovered it themselves. But it has not happened so far. When you have your back to the wall or the Wall Street lunacy, it may not be easy to have a shot at thinking in risky freshness. Someone high in American government recently claimed that we need the automobile industry to do for the 21st century what it did for the 20th: no pause there over the motor madness of ten decades, or some fresh twists on loco-motion.

Later we shall talk about listing the simple facts of business over some period, finding how those facts are interconnected and how they have been badly connected for ten decades, how the story reveals the horrors that resulted, horrors screaming for honest criticism before **we** turn to a basic future perspective that would ground creative policy, open planning, and sane glocal executive reflection.

Have you identified the eight whatever yet?

We shall talk? **We**, chatting now, talking later? **We** must become a force of persuasion that is way beyond the power and character of present lobbying, the dominance of financial manipulators, the stupidities of conventional economics and their world-organizing lackeys. It can no longer be a matter of decent people taking to the streets or NGOs caring gallantly for the global needy and oppressed.

We have to make a start, aligned with the decency hidden in all, so that the decency can be sifted and lifted out of past conventions and brought to the fantasy of a new type of global planning.

I have talked about that new type of planning as grounded in a turn-around. And in its fullness it must be so: next year's holiday experience is to be grist for the holidays to follow. So, the turning is eventually to be a globally taken-for-granted rolling of history forward into a better human future.

In a bright moment musing on this in Montreal at the end of the last century, I came up with a quip, a twist on an old proverb that I used later in writing about such diverse things as economics and linguistic studies: "A Rolling Stone Gathers *Nomos*." *Nomos* is the Greek word for order, and here I am thinking of a creative bent towards the future. Conveniently, *mos* is the Latin for habit, which adds a further twist: we have to avoid gathering *mos*, yesterday's way of living or partly living imported brutally into tomorrow's dreams.

But were tomorrow's dreams not lurking in the moss of yesterday's doings, a molecular reach fermenting in the big bang of 13.7 billion years ago?

Should we not pause over, turn around about, the strange dream mentioned in the last sentence? The book mentioned in note 1 of the "Preface," *The Future as Cultural Fact*, begins on page vii with the statement, "a rolling book gathers a lot of moss," but the rolling of this little book requires luck if we are to dream effectively towards global *Nomos* beyond present *mos*. Don't just wish it luck: make it roll!

CHAPTER 2
EXPRESSING FUTUROLOGY

Would it not be nice to see, and be seized by seeing, the sunflower in the seed? Where is the big bang going? That was the dream-issue and the seed-question fermenting at the end of the previous chapter. Chatting about that will concern us all the way. Here I take an apparently simpler question: what is going where? and I give it a twist of fantasy by taking away the question mark, making it a statement, **what is going where**.

You see that the title here reverses the book-title, and indeed it was the original idea of the book. The book is my effort to express futurology and so to seed a futurology express, a future-running express, a fresh courageous hopefulness that is effective in history.

The freshness, for some an outrageous suspect freshness, comes from inviting a shocking shift in what is called academic history, which has in these recent centuries become a search for a refined patterning of what may be call facts of history. There are the details, be they of battles or villages or parliamentary debates: how are they patterned, or to be patterned? That is not a debate to be entered into here: we slip past Marxist, Whig, whatever, interpretations of history, and past debates about historical method—and, in very imaginative deed we go on a visit to an animal doctor for inspiration.

Certainly we can assume a very rough agreement that, whatever one's heavier philosophy of history or of investigation or of the meaning of the word *reality*, historical knowledge is an expression of historical reality. But now I invite you to take a strange turn by shifting from history to, say, a sick puppy. I bring the sick pup to the vet because the vet has knowledge of dog-reality, and with detection during the visit, there is my hope that there will be forthcoming fresh knowledge and a fresh expression of this pup's reality. But notice the shift of meaning involved. The vet and I both want knowledge, and its expression, that is potentially effective in the pup's well-being.

Here I invite you to reflect on a television series of the past decade named *House*. Even if you have neither heard of it before nor seen it, it does not matter. What matters is that it lifts the vet story into a more complex context. Instead of the sick pup there is a sick human; instead of the vet there is a select group of experts gathered round the genius-type Dr. Gregory House; instead of the regularly standard diagnosis and healing of the vet there is liable, on the show, to be a fermenting towards meeting the case's peculiarities with some creative leaping. But in both cases the result is the same: there is a lift in well-being due to the expression—taken in the very largest practical sense—of the care-giver.

But now you have the question: Is historical knowledge, then, to be turned towards, some would say shrunken into, some practical tunnel, instead of being a reach for, well, for what is really going on, for better or worse, for richer or poorer? This vet-stuff is an all too strange turn against the tide of respectable academic tradition.

We had best go back to the norm of finding out 'what is really going on'. Consider the pup or House's patient: the interest is in what is really going on, but the interest is also in, or rather almost always in, what is going further on. The pup is the concrete possibility of being a dog, and this is the central reason of the investigation of what happened in this dog's past.

By putting the problem that way, we bring ourselves to meet the standard attitude in history head on. What happened to this city in the past? Surely here we see the parallel lost: delving into Beijing's past—Peking under the Mongols, say—has absolutely nothing to do with the city's future goings-on. One is simply asking what went on in Peking in medieval times. There is a panoply of interesting searchings into stonework and diet, defense and conquest, and so on: all building towards a coherent account of what went on in Peking.

What went on in Xanadu (Shangdu) or in the Mongol capital, Karakorum, in the time of Thomas Aquinas? Our problem now is to read this without the question-mark and find that, in the fullness of our interest, we are really interested in, so to speak, a piece of a pup. It brings to my mind my early struggle with this issue, but then my focus was on India, and indeed on the epic containing the *Bhagavad Gita*. Arjuna asks Krishna "what is man?" but I was led by my musings to put in Khrisna's mouth a simple "yes." Yes, what is man; man is **what**; and **what** is going on in ancient India and in medieval Paris and in the Mongol conquests. Does this not nudge towards a changed reading of the end of the previous paragraph: "towards a coherent account of **what** went on in Peking"?

Aggregates of whats went on in Peking or Karakorum or Shangdu. The aggregates were part of the global aggregate of whats, with sub-aggregates patterned as it were from above down, with names like *Mongol,* and each what also, with names like Kublai, a patterning of sub-aggregates that go lower than genetic codes. Are we not here sowing the seed of a turn to the strange parallel of pup, with, say, the pup Kublai so eloquently accounted for in Conn Iggulden's *Conqueror*? Iggulden leaves off his accounting at the end of the book with Kublai Kahn young, if no longer a pup: "For once, I thought, I might finish a series with a character still alive and with all his dreams and hopes to come." What would, what did, Kublai's dreams and hopes effect, what did they sow in Mao's China? Were there dreams that failed that might have tuned Dadu (Beijing) to the rhythm of another drum? Might those dreams be our descendants' dreams, **whats** sown by us?

"Sow What," "So What"? is my problem here, our problem here, and we return to it more patiently in the next chapter. My interest is in your interest in you as **what**. The little word *as* is normally an abstractive word: think of Jane as parent or as pianist. But you as **what** have, in reality, not that meaning. At your best you are all **what**. Our problem is the sowing of fresh seeds of interest in that **what** that you are. But let us put a hold here on that sowing and return to the pup Kublai and his hordes.

Even now, at this early stage in our chatting, you can read Kublai as a what, a reach for achievement, as he rides across the plains of Asia with his following of whats. How well can you thus read him and his wife and son and their reachings? You can read what is going on in the plains of Asia—or in Thomas Aquinas' Paris of the time or in the accounts of those who journeyed between Paris and Karakorum—with a new discontinuous richness, in so far as you have actively turned around the what that you are. Without that turn there can be massively complex patterns, as Toynbee surely shows us, but somehow we whats are left truncated, headless, aheadless.

And it is exactly here that you and I meet together the problem of futurology, of the book, of expressing futurology, of a futurology express. If the story, the history, is to be more than just a register of places and persons and patterns in time, then one has to reach as best one can, in an emergent culture that has an ethos of such reaching, for a grip on the populations of whats going on. Do you genuinely know the sunflower seed when you have only seen the seed or the early shoot? What is ongoing for the listener to the first movement of Mozart's 21st piano concerto if the astonishing next 5+ minutes are missing? Especially if the listener does not know the **what** that is listening?

These are very strange deep questions about your story and mine, about Mozart and Kublai Khan. So back we go to the sunflower shoot or the pup. Is not history a shoot of the aggregate of whats? It goes on as we read and write, an unfinished comedy. We grip its incomplete **what** best in some heuristic grip of its ongoing, even if its tall sunflower smile is in a cloud of unknowing.

But then the pup's future is in a cloud of unknowing for vet and pet-owner. Its journey into that cloud pivots on the vet's present caring interest. Its journey of previous years lurks there for the caring interest to take account of: not then just to ground an account. And that previous journey is only partially detected while the pup still lives; indeed does it not weave through history? And do not the journeys of Kublai Khan weave also through today and through later millennia than ours? Thus "what is going on in Xanadu" looks well beyond the long march of Mao.

History, like the sick pup, is a battered genetic reality. Unlike the sick pup, there have not been previous instances of that genetic reality. (N.B.: "genetic" is here used in the classic sense of *genesis* or development rather than to the more recent meaning relating to genes). We do not know where the macromolecular patterns—nations and narcos—of these times are going, but past micro-patterns twist and turn forward through them in the weave of ancient background radiation.

When we ask "what is going on?" we ask about our own story. We ask about an unknown, a finite shoot. We ask, unknowns, about that unknown, about this single and singular seven-million-year-old fact that is an incomplete pup-fact of aggregates of unknowns with unknown threads searching for future weaves in a search that is dark and sometimes malicious, in a weave that is sometimes a steady weave of cycles of the sickness we name *decline*, decline that we can mistake for progress and call, for recent instances, "the industrial revolution" or "the information explosion."

And in that weave there is the group of whats that are historians, seeking out the goings-on of warriors and sages, weekends and ages, workers and wages. The results of the seeking slide into the weave: should not, then, the story-tellers be careful?

But what does *careful* mean? Again we are back trying to detect the meaning of *what*. We venture into a past jumble of dark facts to ask, "What might these be?" Too easily we miss the fact that 'what might these be?' has a concrete fullness that reaches beyond our present. What might this bronze-age metal be? It might be a rocket to the moon. What, then, is the essence of primitive oxygen? It might be the breath of life.

Before the historian poise flowing facticities, essences primarily unknown. To ask for the essential of that named cluster is to ask for the future. We are living in a tadpole state with little suspicion of the nature of the future frog. What could the question, "What really happened?" mean? What really happened was that the tadpole journeyed on—or was diverted from that journey. Journey to what? The best we can do is detect the genetics up to date, and anticipate a little in that little light. We can do better over ages if there is a sequence of attempts, a sequence of genetic accounts, a genetics of genetic accounts. Best not elaborate further on this, into, for instance, how whatters are to discover statistical probabilities and how these statistics are to penumbrate the genetics and the sequences.

There could be a diseased black-plague butterfly flapping its wings over your grandchild's crib. Would your interest not reach far enough to find a bright idea of the disease's cure in some corner of last century's research? History, then, is not a detached interest in lost ideas.

But leap further: behind an idea is the loneliness of **what** hungry for a piece of the whole story in which that **what** frets and struts. History is the story of immature and cramped lonelinesses, of whats emergent from chemicals in an ancient cosmos. So, it is imperative, and not just interesting, that we remember the future in the remembrance of times past.

Our immaturity cramps our memory in our failure to remember, or rather member, the what that we are. But what could I possibly mean by "membering the what that we are"?

CHAPTER 3
WHAT ARE WE

After two chapters of my turning, you will not have missed the missing question mark in the title of this chapter. So you have suspicions already about where we are going here. Might you rise to think of that going as part, indeed strangely not a part but all, of what we talked of in the previous chapter? We are what, or more precisely an aggregate of whats, and that whatting is a reach for history, for the whole story. The reach may be clouded, battered by parents and schools and media and culture, but it is still there as this print floats past your frontal lobe.

But are we talking now about us, you and me, here and there now? Your question, at least the question I raise here in flat print is, about **what** is still there reading. Only you, **what**, can there answer that in some way beyond stumbling fogginess. And this is true even if you are on the edge of your seat, tuning into yourself in a startling way, wave. Wave! Hello, me!

I recall now, about a decade ago, when I first began to talk of this with fresh edgy personal fulsome meaning, bringing a large proportion of a class of schoolboys to the edge of their seats. It was not that they understood what I was at, what I was getting at, the whats that I was getting at. But they had a sense of something strange, a novel turn in someone talking to them. For some few it was a fresh start to, and in, their school daze; for most it was a sense that became unreal under the battery of the normal flow of the day's schooling. Perhaps you might share the sense in the way it was shared by the few, and go on to knock at the door of your **what** in a way that will, over decades, turn that seed-what into a sunflower-what?

The sense, the tonality, of the classroom took off from a simple exchange between one bright boy and me. I had begun the class by writing on the blackboard—yes, it really was a blackboard, with non-smelly chalk—"What is a schoolboy." The boy's hand called for my attention. "Sir," he said, "you forgot the question-mark." My replay was, as you now expect, that I did not forget: that it was a statement.

We carried on from there in a struggle to genuinely meet as subjects by illustrating the meeting of subjects. A first focus was on the meeting that is a penalty kick in soccer. What we were reaching for was a fuller puzzled sense of the what that was our topic, that is the topic here for you and me. So I pretended that I was the goalkeeper. How was I poised as the taker began the six or seven strides to the ball? I was balanced on my feet, my what in my toes and eyes and fingers. I was all what, molecules in integral mesh. Does that describe you as you read now, a read shaken in the wind of change? Or rather, poised, steady, integrally, in this wind of change? Today Serena Williams was fabulously poised in Wimbledon, winning with shocking ease. (She lost later!) But she was never unpoised in awaiting the other's serve. The what swayed in flexed control, standing on the globe alert to the globe up-tossed and swiped 78 feet away.

Here I am up-tossing print to the back of your eyes: is your **what**, you what, free to toss it on into cranial molecules in disturbing patterns? This is a very existential question. There may be no disturbed patterns, but only the robotic response of stale clusters of molecules, settled into permanent teenage and adult fixity by rote education. Do you meet my print the way you meet well a Ping-Pong ball? Or do you rather meet it the way most people meet Power-Point?

What am I, at my best, if that best has not been bested bit by bit since those early kindergarten days when I was told not to daydream but to pay attention to long-dead adults. Do I—you I mean—have some suspicion of that besting? Sometimes, when I am in one of the science libraries of UBC—a local Vancouver university—I sadly watch busy students highlighting textbooks as they move through the rites that are the wrongs of higher education. Far, far away is the mood of the Korean poetess, Kim Hyesoon (I quote the translation by Don Mee Choi): "Someone is taking out / a question from a question mark. / Question that flew like a chicken feather, / question that gave its body to the wind, / question that stripped naked, / question that painted the entire body."

So instead of the best there is, as norm, the worse. We become fodder for pseudo-democracy. There is the old Russian joke: "What is capitalism?" "It is the oppression of man by man." "And, comrade, what is communism?" "It is the reverse." But the question about, the what in, the whats in, democracy, will occupy us later. Or will it? What is it for a question to occupy us, me and you, "question that stripped naked / question that painted the entire body"? Were it thus we would indeed be keeping the goal of education. But the question of education is one that should occupy us all cyclically later: if whats beat the bestings.

Meantime let us muse, sense, ponder, lesser things. My favorite pondering in lecturing to young ladies at a university in a former life—that lasted twenty years—was a shared and entertaining pondering about the dates they regularly risked on Friday evenings. Indeed, often we bantered in class on Friday about possibilities and on Monday groaned over actualities. What are the possibilities? Rather, I should write, as we usually spoke in class, "**What** is the possibility." We assumed, for convenience, that the possibility was male, although a decent percentage of the ladies were gay. Take the illustration, as I describe it now, to some encounter of your own. The advantage of following it thus is that, as the old adage has it, it is easier to spy the other's mote, or motives!

Sometimes I shared the university bus with my lady-students on the way to their downtown meeting places. The bus vibrated with anticipations as well, of course, as with a spectrum of scents. Our musings on Friday would be about anticipations, but now the musers head towards focusing on the fellow already perhaps two beers up, or might I say, down? Is the fellow like Serena Williams, poised for whatever his companion serves? *Whatever* here covers a range of servings, a range common to all humanity, and it is best, though impossibly compact, to display that range in a diagrammatic form. I do so at the end of this chapter. Reading those diagrams: that, as we'll come to see, is the task of a millennium. But let us sniff our way into the topic with the Friday-night adventurers. Sniff? The perfumed lady enters: does the guy notice the change of air? Is he attentive to the aesthetic patterns that pace into his presence? Attention is the first zone of whatting: literally sensing where the friend, companion, opponent, is coming from. Think of the parallel in tennis or soccer. And it is also the zone of aesthetic openness.

But the core of whatting is a reach for understanding. Is the dated fellow that reach? "How are you?" he says, but what is the extent of that reach in him? Sadly, it can be almost an empty verbal reflex and can echo thus in the lady's ear. And there is that other level of what: "What might you be this evening? What might we do together?" Has the chap—call him Cosmo—got adventure in his core, his cor, his heart? Or does he just want to get laid?

There are new books to be written, and new roads and buildings to be formed, to warm up that heart of you in new ways. Here you and I are only tip-toeing through the tulips, the true lips of what-questing. And that tip-toeing can echo the sadness of the dating lady: "Is this guy really reaching for the embrace of understanding and adventure?" Our class of Monday morning was all too often a homecoming to a sad realism that the **what** he is was a shrunken shadow of his childhood reach. The culture of *The Lonely Crowd* that Riesman wrote of fifty years ago, and Paul Simon sang of, is not just still there, but worse. "People talking without speaking, people hearing without listening"? Now

Cosmo is likely to be in the cell of his cellphone, staying out of touch.

Nor does the flow of self-help books, asking for stillness, give the answer to being out of touch. The what-muscle that is me needs to climb through simple exercises to be able to meet the servings, good or bad, of this day of history's game, history's twisting invitations to sunflower, to global freshness.

I end here with diagrams that we have, yes, touched on, that might have touched us. This is us, you and I, but can we come to recognize the road to recognize our selves? These are maps of a road not travelled. Do not mistake map-reading of the mountain that is you for the climb that you might be.

Dynamics of Knowing

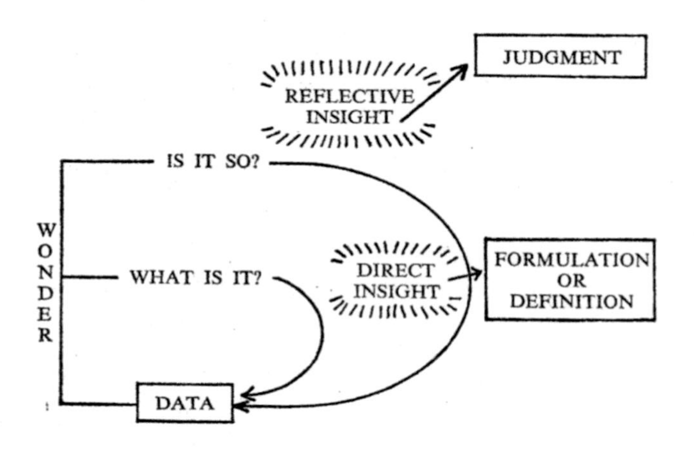

Dynamics of Doing

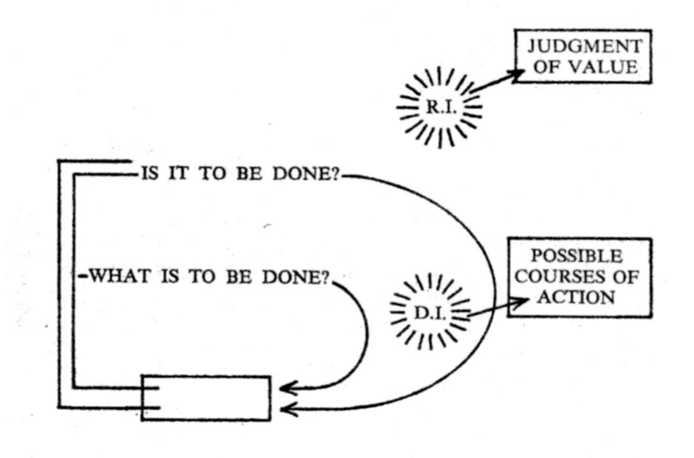

CHAPTER 4
WHAT RESCUES FUTUROLOGY

Or is futurology to rescue what? There is the oddity that the move forward is a two-way stretch. I have named, in the last few pages, the **what** that is you or I, and here I turn to name the turn-around that is an eight-fold rolling of global goings-on. It was fragmentarily introduced for a family but now is to be stretched to the millions of years of humanity's squatting whatting in the ancient bang of molecules, whirling home.

I write of a two way stretch or a two-way rescuing. There is a very sound sense in which futurology, as I skimpily describe it in this chapter, is to rescue **what**. This means that this chapter can be a fresh start. If you are reading through the book speedily, bursting with curiosity or even just impatient to find the answer to the question, "What does this guy suggest that futurology is?" then you really have not yet got to grips with what **what** is, but nonetheless you can roll on comfortably here and even come to nod at the plausibility of the cyclic structure that I outline.

Furthermore, you may find the structure to be something strangely, or not at all strangely, familiar. Are you a student of literature? Then you will notice, if you pick up such a classic as Wellek and Warren's *Theory of Literature*, that the chapter divisions in the table of contents resemble the divisions that I suggest. What may be novel is the cyclic connecting, turning a list of eight different functions into a cyclic list, the last leading naturally to an input to the first. But let me lay out the list for you, just as a list: *Research, Interpretation, History, Dialectic, Foundations, Doctrines, Systematics, Communications.*

If you think back to the dysfunctional family and the suggested activities you will recognized the eight components. They are called *functional* simply because they **function** in the sequence in which I listed them. You may not be a student of literature but of some other zone in art, science, technology, law, or you may have a hobby that you might think about in terms of the list. My own first leap from the list to the reality of its seeds and its necessity was a memorable afternoon in the Old Bodleian Library in Oxford in the summer of 1969. I was sitting in the meager section—a dozen or so shelves—that dealt with music and musicology. I had the list in my head, but as I mused over the collection of books and journals—I recall especially working on the journal *Perspectives of New Music*—it dawned on me that the muddles represented by the global interest in music and its study that were expressed there cried out for the order that, till then, I had not thought of as relating to the realms of the aesthetic. A decade later I moved into the culture of dancing to discover the same need. For me, as for Susanne Langer, dance is a more radical reality and I find it curious to note—I would hope you would too—that in a visit to Oxford a few years ago, the cinemas were bursting with new dance films, but neither the Bodleian nor the various book stores had much to offer regarding dance. It seems to me that it is a life pattern and art form at the heart of our loneliness and the potential of that loneliness, yet older traditions of learned discourse list dance's circling round the sacred as lower on their totem pole. In contrast, the small collection with which I worked in music has emigrated by now to the New Bodleian, where it shares abundant space with such areas as economics and—in wondrous upper space and perspective!—Indian Studies.

I ramble thus to nudge you to let your what stray and expand, perhaps in your work place, perhaps in a library. You are on **the base** (*al quaeda*) line or you are in the goal, and what is being served to you has inviting subtleties of ... return of serve. People made pins long before pin-factories: what, now, of the works of the pen? What now of the works of governing, be it that of corporations or nations? And what of your hobbies? Do you, for instance, climb? My family has an interest in that zone, and recent ventures of mine into its culture and literature show that same unordered set reaching round about the question, "What is climbing?" "What is climbing?" can take serious mind-climbing shape with the benefit of this cyclic collaboration. Think, then, of the turn given by dropping the question mark. What is climbing, is singing, is reading Chinese or Celtic or African literature. Surely we would be better off if we appreciated the **what** we are doing? The division suggested is simple and almost primitive. We are going from the past to the future. We are being served from the past and present and so often we miss the wonders of the shot at the future.

But on the larger scale there is the problem of having a future that is not a descent of humanity but an ascent: there, indeed, lurks the global ecological problem. Much of this book (as you will later see) focuses on the gross mess of economic non-science, but my fuller interest is in the crisis that is upon us now, and not just something we associate with such a year as 2050 A.D. Stewart Brand writes of that year as a sort-of beginning of lost-chance. We can witness people wearing masks in Singapore and Mumbai, in Manila and Birmingham. Brand's stand is clear: "Whether it is called saving the commons, niche-construction, ecosystem engineering, mega-gardening, or intentional Gaia, humanity is now stuck with a planet stewardship role." Stewart Brand,*Whole Earth Discipline: An Ecopragmatist Manifesto* (New York: Viking, 2010), 275. And before him there was the appeal of Arne Naess in "Deep Ecology and Ultimate Premises" (*The Ecologist*, vol. 18, 1988), an appeal that amazingly sensed the need for functional collaboration.

I draw on my own ramble only that you too might pause and ramble over the larger problems in your own life or in the global misery of senseless wars, senseless crop-structurings, senseless food-tradings. I ask you for a minimal response but with a sting in the tale. The minimal response to the question, "Does this division make sense?" is, "Yes, it does." The sting in the tale that is you reading what I write of my tale and the global tale is the seeding in your **what** of "What might I do about it?" Talk about it just does not cut it **unless** it becomes functional. Dysfunctional talk is abundant: there is a steady flow of talk in journals and twitters, in coffee-shops and pubs, in government papers and academic research. How is it to become functional and effective? Only if the drive to implementing good ideas becomes effective. How can this effectiveness be achieved? The question leads back to musing about the list already given. It names something that does not yet exist, a new type of thinking and talking that is to become a global power, perhaps before the tenth millennium. I myself have identified, and nudge you to identify, zones that show that need. But we do not have the reality, only the fantasy based on that zone-showing.

Forget the sting in the tale and muse over the plausibility as one sitting on the fence, an observer of history. Suggested are eight connected groupings. Think of the last three groups listed: a group that focus on the generation of sane policy; a group that thinks out various patterns in which the policies can become realities; a group that selects locally relevant policies through creative meshing of such patterns with local patterns of life. There you have it: the old trio of policy, planning, and executive reflection, to which must be added a further set of groups—call them C_9—whose common sense resonates with the whole ethos of functional care.

And perhaps it is the cultivation of that ethos that is the basic hope of this little work. But let me note immediately regarding that old trio made fresh and its output, that there is no difficulty in recognizing its limitations and its fallibility. As Robby Burns put it, the best laid schemes of human beings "gang aft agley" (or, for those of a less severe Scottish-Gaelic tilt and lilt, "go oft awry"). But the partial success and the patterns of failure are for recycling from the village or classroom or bank or wherever the failures, the stumblings, occur. The recycling is from perhaps a single instance or village in which the anomaly of failure is noticed and identified within the ethos that I talk about. But I must note that the ethos changes as the work enters *The Tower of Able*, as I call it. The ethos of functional collaboration does not require of common sense that it become the uncommon sense that is gripped in a self- and phyletic- luminousness of the caring. What I mean by the "luminousness of caring," well, we'll go round that again several times in this little book: particularly in chapters 11, 16 and 17, and in a fuller fashion in chapter 20 and the Epilogue. But notice that the "round that again" is a deliberate choice of words that relates to the ongoing genesis of the functional collaboration.

The attempt to go round it in a fleeting first is what we did together in chapter one. The first attempts in any area will necessarily be stumbling attempts. Slowly the Tower, the Lighthouse, will rise. What do I mean by rise? I mean that it will rise above common sense, however rich and aesthetic, towards a shared deep personal understanding that is scientific in a best and indeed quite new sense. This new sense is to be wildly different from the present strangely detached way that prevails of going about serious study. So for instance, in zoology it will integrate pet, pup, patient, patient-helping, possibilities, within a neuro- and eco-chemistry of appreciation, classification, and cherishing. It will be nearer the aboriginal respect for animals than the labors of laboratories.

But the new sense that I speak of belongs in the self-creating up-spiraling of "The Tower." The end of the last paragraph is merely my reach to common sense at its best, a best that senses that somehow we have cut ourselves off from the vibes of evolution: so we find ourselves discovering, in recent decades, that dogs have a place in hospitals and psychic distress.

I ramble thus, because what is important at this initial stage is plausibility and mood. How can we possibly educate the zoologist towards genuine animal understanding? In my days of teaching undergraduate philosophy of science, I used to point out that Konrad Lorenz got a Nobel Prize in the 1970s for finding out that zoology was about live animals. In the local university departments the only live animal that most of my students encountered in their studies was the fruit fly.

Back now to the cyclic work of eight groups. We have mused a little over the last three. Think now of the first three. They are very evident in present physics: a large group, competent in the Standard Model, brood endlessly over the factual output of cyclotronic spinning to pitch up anomalies to the group of first-rate theorists. The theorists patch up the Standard Model, or perhaps move off on a dangerously unempirical limb like string theory. How dangerous? The task of sniffing the danger has to be picked up more seriously by a group with better roots in history.

I have left the two central tasks of dialectic and foundations to a concluding comment. They are precise topics of a cluster of later chapters, beginning with a quite slow ramble round the dialectic task in chapters 8, 9, and 10, the achievement of which leads to foundations people, foundations people already poised in the turn to the future. But note that what we have been at and about in this chapter is a popular dense form of these complex group activities leading to your foundations. I wish for you, **what**, to get a foundational sniff of the foundations of futurology. My effort to do so is this twisting and turnings of words. It turns you and me in a slow—the pace is now yours—dialectic ramble that can be, has been, is to be, a mix of confusions, aggravations, and delights.

Chapter 5
Listing Simple Economic Facts

The simplest present economic fact would seem to be that we, globally, are in an economic mess. Something like our Toronto family after twenty years of shabby holidaying at the lakeside. Should we do something like their turn-around and have a shot at finding out what is going-on and going wrong? Make an initial list of .... of **what**, I nearly wrote, indeed did write, there now, front and end of dotty writing, of **what** .... But, yes, you are familiar with the implied list and how we have been down that trail already and, I hope, you now smile at the idea of a list of Tom, Dick and Mary, Misha and Erimumba, Xenrios and Irina etc.: the seven billion economic whats on our present globe.

I suppose we could get going listing the facts about sub-divisions of this global population, but are not the horrors of these divisions all too familiar? At the economic bottom the billion below the capability of purchasing a decent living; at the thin top, the billionaires. Then there is the population of pundits: ministers of finance, governors of banks, etc. and their groupings, G_8, G_{12}, G_{east} G_{south}, whatever, and those other groupings like World Bank, IMF, etc. These are groupings of whats whose whats are no longer up to—never were up to—the game, whose whats are immersed in assumptions and arrogances, without much suspicion of the simple economic fact that the right list is somehow missing, and that even if such a list appeared their whats and their hearts are just not in it, not in the right mood. I ended a recent volume of the Indian Journal *Divyadaan* (vol. 21, no. 2 [2010]) titled "Do you want a sane global economy?" with the comment:

> The spirit of inquiry, the heart of serious science, is just not present either in contemporary economic establishment economics or in the range of views opposed to it. So, neither group takes seriously the quest for real basic variables. Such seriousness has to emerge

from a creative minority, towards which this volume reaches. The creativity demanded is the coming to grips with the dynamics of any business and the drawing attention to it.

The absence of seriousness is a more conventional way of talking about dead whats and whatters. Coming to grips, in that arrogantly dead population, with the dynamics of any business seems, then, out of the question. Ho, ho: get that, "out of the question"? In other words, beyond the reach of the contemporary **what**.

But surely, like the dysfunctional family, there can be a start with listings? The trouble with this is that there was a false start with listing much more than a century ago that is now the thriving business of statistics, but the statistics are way off base. Furthest off base are the statistics associated with stock exchanges that are pitched at us mindlessly in the newses of all nations. These have—even the great Lord Keynes admitted it—almost nothing to do with real business. What of the lists in the financial sections of papers? They are like off-track betting reports.

So we are worse off than the dysfunctional family regarding facts. I suppose I might go back to chemistry before 1790 and Lavoisier's discovery of oxygen, back to listings tied in with phlogiston, to get a sense of muddled listings. But more familiar and easier is a paralleling with physics in the past century. Listings emerged of the particles that are the object of the science of physics, and those lists became bafflingly complex. It took some quite decent creative leaping to get us out of the mess and on to the very plausible control of what is called *The Standard Model*. Then the previous messy lists made sense, leaving openings for further creative empirical leaping; indeed, leaving openings for the non-empirical leaping of String Theory, which catches the public imagination.

In present economic thinking there is an abundance of non-empirical leaping out there, suavely stringing us along. But perhaps I can admit that I was not entirely honest when I claimed that such leaping was "without much suspicion of the simple economic fact that the right list is somehow missing." In the first half of 2013 there were some amazing admissions of ignorance exposed by different media. Top bankers became frank about the factual shakiness of their so-called money-printing. Heads of government in Europe admitted that they met to seek solutions with quite different listings of problems and solutions. Do I need to ramble back to the financial leapings of the past decade, whether disguised as boostings or bail-outs? The arrogant ignorant messing continues, and Wall Street stands firmer than the Berlin Wall of forty years ago. It will take more than sit-ins or even riots to shake the money-gamers. But what will it take? Yes, it will take **what**, your what, our what, our human family whats. And, like that small Toronto family, we need some relevant lists to get us started.

But, alas, there is the relevant list to be leaped to, and, alas again, when the leap is made and named, in its startling simplicity, the number crunchers of the past century will deny that it is relevant: "have we not a hugely complex economics to point to, with its almost predictive statistics?" Indeed, a huge part of our trouble is the arrogance of an erroneously predictive statistics that leaves our national and international financing in the hands of well-suited casino players.

But I have wandered from our simple problem of listing simple economic facts. I have remarked that the listing takes a creative leap, and to help you on with the wonder and simplicity of that leap I go back to Isaac Newton under the legendary apple tree, looking up, in some paintings of the legend, at an apple with the moon beside it. He lived at that time in a culture of mythic listing of two types of objects. The apple is of earth; the moon is up there on the edge of quintessential beings. The apple falls; the moon does not.

But now Isaac joins the goalkeeper and Serena Williams as he poises, not on his feet but on his bottom, before the round served objects, and becomes a radiant molecular **what**. The list of two types of objects shrinks, in his mind's what, to one. The "shrinking in his mind's what" is, I suspect, rather baffling to you? And I would note that your bafflement was slow-shared by Newton on one level, but not shared at all on another. For the whole business—a matter of weeks in his study not minutes under a tree—was spontaneous for him. He, like Archimedes 2,000 years before him, was an astounding whatter, but nonetheless, only spontaneously so. Some evidence for this untutored spontaneity is to be found in the two great works of the pair. Have a run at Archimedes' *On Floating Bodies*, or Newton's *Principia*, and note the brilliant men's failure to help us along with the shrinking. Understanding how the shrinking is done by what, and understanding with precision how to help others grasp the shrinking, that was beyond them.

At all events, the apple and the moon find their way into the same list, obeying a universal law of travel. But what has this got to do with our economic listings, and the search for a relevant list to break us out of this century's astronomical economic problems?

So now I invite you to think of another chap of the same period as Newton but bent on being industrious: let us call him (in those times, ladies were not invited into the indelicacies of business) Smith or Adam or some such. He is, perhaps, not under a tree but poised in front of trade: the to and fro of buying and selling. There is a flow of goods of all sorts to behold, with coins and bills flowing the other way. It is an amazing mixed flow, but still a single flow. It needs to be measured, controlled, and indeed a hundred years later there is the achievement—may I mention Leon Walras?—of getting the whole thing of the market into a vast set of equations of equilibrium. No need to go on here, since I wish only to note that there we have a reversal of Newton's problem, which was to jump from two types of things in reality's flow to a single type. Smith and Walras and the circus of lazy or trapped **whats** that followed them settle for the single obvious flow. Oh, yes, there are such things as capital goods, but we can take the measure of them, even if a very bright woman like Joan Robinson laughs at our muddled measures and our eventual wobbling equilibriums. We shall come back to that laugh later.

The point of my ramble and the parallels is that a Newtonian jump is needed to get the initial simple facts straight. It is not as complex as Einstein's jumps, or Schrödinger's, in physics, but it seems beyond the minds of present economists. We could pause over this business of presuppositional advantages or handicaps for a whole book, for it is key to the future of futurology, but let us stick with the main point for the moment. Some leaping is needed to identify simple relevant economic facts. Old habits of listing, especially accompanied by barrels of fishy statistics posing as science, hold **whats** hostage. So, government finance gurus juggle interest rates, invent money, watch the casino, and—even if they do honestly try ignorant legislations of control—let the jugglers of money as commodity have their destructive day.

We have, then, the present situation of established ignorance both of the basic variables and of the norms of their financing. There is no sense in trying to handle this global mess in this short work. What I do instead is patch in leads and hints of directions to be taken and exercises to be done that help both to make a small beginning of lifting oneself into the new contexts both of the simple shifts of Economics 101 and of the huge shifts required by the futurology that is the eightfold functional collaboration. Only very slowly and incompletely do I open up the topic of the full effort required to get us forward to a humane global care. A first entry into the task—save it, perhaps, till you have finished a first read of the book, but take time now to find that the task is not easy—is to simply view the standard diagrams of present first-year courses in economics. I conclude with two such diagrams. Can you spot the flaws? That indeed would be some achievement for a beginner here. Nurse the confusion and the mess till you read the conclusion of chapter 7.

The two diagrams that follow are from Philip McShane, *Economics for Everyone: Das Jus Kapital* (Halifax, Axial Press, 1998), pages 32 and 33.

A SIMPLE IMAGINARY ECONOMY

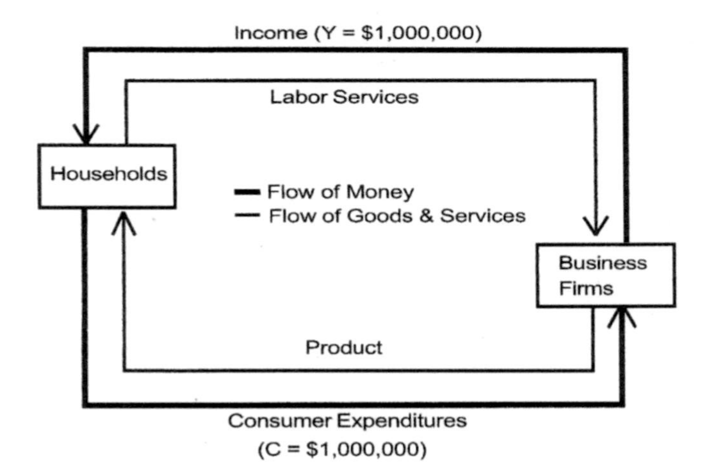

The Circular Flow of Income and Consumer Expenditures
The circular flow of income and expenditure in a simple imaginary economy in which households consume their entire income. There aare no taxes, no government spending, no saving, no investment, and no foreign sector.

SAVING LEAKS OUT OF THE SPENDING STEAM BUT REAPPEARS AS INVESTMENT

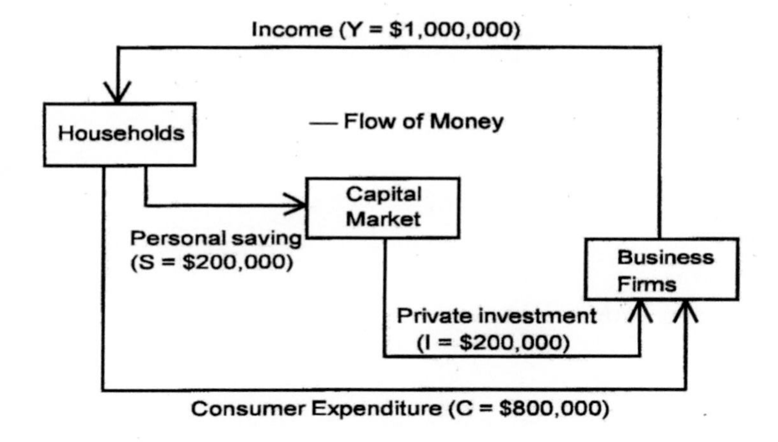

Chapter 6
Interpreting Facts

Scientific types among you may find it odd that I do not begin from such a title as "interpreting data." I seem to be biasing the expression oddly in favor of the division of labor suggested already. But data, literally—from Latin—what are given in science or any discourse indeed, are within a type of talking that says, "this is odd," "this is an anomaly." Common sense can recognize an anomaly and seek out the doctor or the mechanic. Common sense recognizes that the relevant expert has know-how. What common sense does not easily recognize is that the really good expert has an understanding of the know-how, and that such understanding is what is needed to handle a serious oddity, anomaly, and indeed is generally not enough for the job. This itself seems an oddity, doesn't it? One normally goes to the doctor or the vet with the oddity of the patient or pup, and one comes away with decent directives regarding health.

But the oddity can be something like the oddities that Dr. House handles with the back-up of his team, an oddity that is off-beat and needs a creative stumbling such as the television program *House* often illustrated. Off-beat? It does not fit into current understanding or current know-how. It may even call for a paradigm shift. The latter is true of present economics and its harmful flow into business, banking, government—and, indeed, following that needed shift round the full cycle to a salvation of democracy was one of my early plans for this little book. It was dropped because it gradually revealed itself as narrowing the scope of our vision of futurology.

That notion of narrowing the vision by focusing on solving what seems to be the major social sickness of time—at the root of poverty, pollution, and political nonsense—would seem to be a very odd notion of narrowing. But, in the first place, the solution is not a matter of me identifying it in a book: that identification has been done unsuccessfully decades ago. It is a matter of involving people like you in seeding various parts of the infant cycling, and doing so in your own zone of interest, which may be quite remote from the economic mess. So it is better to write here in a manner that helps you to see that "my zone is in a mess," to see an oddity in your own zone.

But there is a twist in my strategy here, a back-to-the-wall twist: the oddity is you, the zone is you as you interpret. We are back to you as what, of course, but now as interpreting something simple, or at least apparently simple. I think, as I move into my simple puzzle about ups and downs, of the title of a favorite book, *The Rise and Fall and Rise of Modern Dance*, a topic that indeed could have dominated this book. I think of the ups and downs of the economy, business cycles. I think of ups and downs in life, or daily mood-swings. So now I write two lines, one above one below:

A E F ....

B C D ....

The puzzle for you, represented by the dots, is where to put the rest of the alphabet, up or down? The problem is, to find the law of division that I am using here. But the deeper problem here is to find out how you find out. That problem is the problem of our present culture, globally. It varies with culture and with age. It is the problem of finding the dynamics of what-development, whether ontic or phyletic. What I am doing here is applying *The Childout Principle* to our climb: "When teaching children geometry, one is teaching children children." I sometimes call that Principle by the neat name *COPON*. I wish, as I write or teach, for you to interpret you while you interpret something, anything, and this wish is the core wish relevant to the breakthrough to luminous futurology. Luminous futurology is, if you like, cyclic COPON. So, here I wish you to do something quite small, now or later. You need to seriously pause, and meet this turn "head on": are you, implicitly, going to spring the same stunt as Namaan the leper did (2 *Kings,* 5:12): "I have larger enterprises in my home zone"? A disciple of mine recently placed the puzzle in a lengthy outline of a doctorate thesis; the three readers moved gaily past it.

I will return to this challenge in its startling fullness in chapter 20, but in fact it is the turn-around that haunts this book about us having our backs to the wall. It recalls Descartes' conviction that many people felt it beneath them to direct their efforts to apparently trifling problems. It recalls Newton's apparently trifling problem of two types of bodies. It recalls the two types of firms that economist consider too trifling a distinction to pause over, a failure that is destroying our global economy and the grounds of trusting each other.

What do I do when I interpret successfully? Well, suppose I wrote out the answer to the ABC puzzle here. You would most likely nod your way past a successful interpretation. The brutal fact of our culture is the mistaking of technical competence for intelligent control. So governments and bankers and economists talk about interest-rate strategies to handle economic ups and downs. Your doctor or shrink, after some little technical talk about your ups and downs, may write you a prescription. The great thing about modern dancing is that you cannot bullshit your way to apparent success: the interest-rate is your incarnate interest-rate, the prescription is sweaty self-involvement way beyond method-acting.

So: why not pause for a bit of childlike fun? On occasion *getting there,* in my up and down puzzle, even with my help, can take a couple of humbling hours. My help usually is a matter of adding letters one by one, even to the end of the alphabet and then going beyond that into funny little pictures.

What is it to interpret simple significant—now there is an added significant word on which I do not comment!—facts? It is to be poised, as relaxedly as possible, to break with your present view. A standard model works O.K. until such-and-such oddity is found by a research group: it may take a generation of physicists to interpret the oddity into a new standard model that gives the oddity an obviousness. The shift also, of course, provides techniques for the less bright, especially if it is presented with symbolic suggestiveness. More on that in chapter 16.

Should I add some more letters to the puzzle? Rather, let me merely say that the last five letters of the alphabet go on top. Write them in: now what about you!!?

I have been talking about interpretation here as picking up on research that is functional, that in other words is poised to hand out oddities to another community of specialists. So, you, as interpreter, seem here to be orientated towards the research, a past achievement. But your bent, in so far as you are incarnately in the cyclic culture, is to so interpret as to hand out a fresh understanding to those who struggle with concretely ongoing meaning. In its fullness interpretation means being in the full cycle of getting relevant meaning to be effective in the historical process. Oddly, this applies as much to poetry and it does to physics, and might I give you a turn, by saying that, that odd saying can lift you to a fresh integral view of the cycling process?

But there is a further more elementary point to be made that is enormously important at this stage. Think back to the group of expert doctors or vets that we mused about in chapter 2: In the *House* television show there emerged regularly different opinions. What followed were intelligent exchanges that compared, not the different opinions, but those opinions with the best integral perspective on the reality. This is an extremely important aspect of serious cycling that needs ingesting, whether in philosophy or economics. There is altogether too much useless mileage to be got out of comparing opinions: Jones and Smith on X. Who was it who remarked that she longed to meet a one-handed economist?! At any rate, as we'll see better in chapter 8, *Comparison* is a key operation in the fourth specialty, Dialectic, but it is a mood that haunts the whole collaboration. Two or three research opinions on oddities had best be confronted with the Standard Model before passing on the task of improvement of the human lot to interpreters.

Dare I point to further complexities? They relate to studies called the history of ideas, and the instance of such study on my mind at the moment—we are heading to consider concrete history—is a massive book by that great Austrian Joseph Schumpeter on the story of economic ideas. Surely, you may say, this problem is a topic for the next specialty. But, as the effort to establish futurology matures, it will become quite clear that the history of ideas is part of the Standard Model, part, then, of the poise of the interpreters. Think again of the *House* group of doctors, one of which was a Chinese lady. Could she not come up with a new twist on an old view in Chinese medicine? Well she could if she had *Remembrance of Things Past* in a way quite beyond Proust.

Further, the luminous remembrance of times past is to be integral, the same powerful perspective in all areas, even if its luminousness is more radiant in the person's particular interest. The choreographer had best not ignore medicine; the doctor cannot be ignorant of gesture: the coach in any area needs, not just knowledge of players, pitches, games, but the story of ideas, including odd untried ideas like scoring a soccer goal by rotating backward, or returning a strange tennis shot through a one-hand stand.

And now you may claim that my shot here is strange, for I seem to be pushing for both a grip on the history of ideas and a serious grip on history. Yes, that is the push: it is the push of the cycling, or perhaps I should say, its pull? The mature global collaboration is to have a shared explanatory richness, an incarnate meaning for the slogan *A Rolling Stone Gathers Nomos*. Functional collaboration pivots on dodging the dysfunction of tunnel-visioned specialization by the paradoxical integration of a full historical heuristic with a precisely tuned functional task. But now, yes, I am dancing into the realms of fantasy, leaving the fixed steps of nineteenth century Russian Ballet to leap way beyond *The Rites of Spring*.

Best to conclude with some musing on our little exercise of interpretation. You still haven't tackled it? No time like the present. But do note that you can share the suffering. My focal interest here is in giving some impression, or expression, of the circuit from researcher to interpreter to historian etc. But there is a common type of talk that could occur in 2014, a tuning to the Childout Principle, the COPON principle, that might hit this street or, this school or that. It is a Principle that lifts the strategy of Socrates towards new culture, the strategy of discovering our communal nescience. That communal nescience is brutally and sickeningly present now, unacknowledged the world and word over. It is disgustingly arrogant. It is challenged here by the apparently simple puzzle, "How are the two types of firm related?" Amazingly, the solution to the business ups-and-downs pivots on the solution to the simple puzzle. There is a list of famous people—including Karl Marx—who struggled unsuccessfully with the ups-and-downs puzzle and the inequalities that go with it. The chap I mentioned earlier, Schumpeter, did better than Marx in interpreting the puzzling rhythms of business, with a little book early in the twentieth century and two big volumes on *Business Cycles* in 1939, when Keynes and Hicks weaved their simple-mindedness into the war's solution to the problem. It brings to mind a saying of H.L. Mencken: "There is always an easy solution to every human problem: neat, plausible, and wrong." The untidy, implausible, and correct solution is to hand. Can we get it to head? It will, no doubt, come to a head, even perhaps to heads of state, when the economic disasters that plague the globe at present pollute radically the waters of power and production. But the spectre is there, a shared arrogant dullness of whatting that is the central component both of the governing establishments and of those who oppose them. We have moved forward to a horrendous deepening and twisting of what Marx talked of in the opening words of his *Communist Manifesto,* "A spectre is haunting Economics—the spectre of communism. All the powers of old Economics have entered into a holy alliance to exorcise this spectre: Pope and Tsar, Meternich and Guizot, French Radicals and German policemen." The spectre now is Futurology, and I wish this little manifesto to bring it hauntingly into your mind, the spectre of a luminously revolutionary interpretation of interpretation and of human survival.

CHAPTER 7
THE ONGOING ECONOMIC HELLIDAY

Two stories interest me here, with dates bracketing the twentieth century by fifteen years each end: there is the glorious story of the expansion of dance movements at the end of the nineteenth century; there is the disgusting story of the downward spiral of apparent economic successes at the end of the twentieth century. The two stories have different darknesses. I think of Merce Cunningham's remark about dance in a 1989 interview on BBC: "Each day it remains just as unknown as when I started." It is such unknowing that we must live in if we are to flesh forth futurology. But we cannot live thus unless we climb into it by humble little steps of educcatering **what**. To Cunningham's remark I add the comment of that great lady, George Eliot: "As it is, the quickest of us walk about well wadded with stupidity." (I quote from the 1977 Norton edition of her 1874 novel, *Middlemarch*, page 135.) The economic and political thinking of the twentieth century has been well wadded with stupidity.

In chapter eleven we will view freshly **what's** rescuing of the future in the seeding and shooting and saplinking of futurology, but it is best to be coldly alert to the global fact of a firm, relentless stand against reaching for appreciation, for limb-changing insights. Might I throw in a third story of interest: the gloomy story of mindless memorization in education? In two decades of university courses in which I was teaching young ladies the elements of their battered selves, I communicated that death of **what** with the simple exercise of getting them to go to the university book store at the beginning of the year and check the indices of textbooks used in the different departments that dealt with children: child studies, psychology, children's literature (or, as it was called, kiddy lit), and a range of sub-departments in education. The indices of these texts—are you even slightly outraged?—had nothing much under *Q*, except Questionaire,

Quine, and such. Indeed sometimes there was nothing in the index between *pubic hair* and *rats*. Most recently I found an index where there was nothing under Q, but between *purification* and *racism* there was *Al Qaeda*. (The book is the one I refer to occasionally here: *The Future as Cultural Fact*). Notice the paradox, if you translate "Al Qaeda": what was present and absent at the same time in the index is The Base. The Base is the Question.

Do I rant? The difference in the ranting and the story-telling here is that in this back-to-the-wall madness I offer a radically different Al Qaeda, a concrete turn-around project that is to be effective in the long run. Who would ever dream of a climb to a radically different world sub-community that would, literally, threaten big government, big business, big evil? Lucky Luciano was famed for his organization of organized crime. His unity of families and his commission was claimed by some historians to be an opposition government in the U.S. So, the wartime control of the Atlantic docks fell to Luciano in jail, for which his reward was being let out of jail to go home, where he got into control of the heroine trade. Might I—or rather the old guy in Toronto, a contemporary of Lucky—be lucky enough to be recognized as seeding the organization of disorganized good-will?

Yet the organization is not to be bureaucratic, but free-moving like so much of the best of contemporary dance. What form is that non-bureaucracy to take? That is a puzzle like the simple puzzle of the last chapter. It is the puzzle of democracy that has been around for at least four millennia. As the global riots intimate, no present structure solves it; such structures in our times are often the plaything and offspring of the military-industrial complex and the stupid and greedy management of sciences, arts, work, sex, and joy. It brings to mind a slogan written on a wall in Belfast during the troubles of the past century: "Is there a life before death?"

But the purpose of my nudging here is to bring our whats on into the lonely need to rewrite the last century's history with dark accuracy. That is a task of this century's futurology. Meantime, there is the task of seeding that transformation by some people pushing towards a stumbling invention of functional history. But I would note that the transformation is not a rejection of the old Ranke slogan, *"wie es eigentlich gewesen,"* it is a facing of the fact, the facts, of history as centrally desire and loneliness. There are subtle clues from the story of dancing and there are unsubtle clues from the stupidity and cupidity that surrounds economic thinking, a thinking that pollutes our air and our minds, our musics and our moneys, our governments and our daily unnecessary grinds.

I mentioned, a page back, the possibility of doing for the globe something like Lucky Luciano did for organized crime, but might I hope that Richard Branson would eventually break forward to that honor? He has been on the job for a decade now, setting up the equivalent of Luciano's commission with odd bods like Bono and Bishop Tutu. Now it is a more respectable group called "Team B," with members like Jochen Zeitz. They are pushing to work out a Plan B. Today, indeed, June 24th 2013, as I continue writing this chapter, I find the report of an address of Arianna Huffington that fits in with our struggle in that it allows me to draw your attention to some tragically bad interpretation and history. Arianna's claim, and the group's, is that "there's more to business than profit." (The report was posted on the CBC News web site on June 14th, 2013 and it is available at: http://www.cbc.ca/news/world/story/2013/06/19/profit-corporate-social-responsibility-b-team.html). Well said. But then she goes on later to say "that there is nothing intrinsically wrong with capitalism." There, alas, she is in the flow of a traditional non-science that pretends economic understanding. Opposing her there is Professor Daniel Altman of New York University who says that abandoning the pure profit model would be a huge mistake. "We should encourage companies to continue doing what they do well, focusing on profit, but in the long term. I think that what the B Team is saying is internally contradictory because in the long term what's good for companies is good for people and the planet. The profit motive is enough." Tell that to the long-term poor and hungry of these past centuries!

The to and fro, which has been a pseudo-scientific debate through the past 150 years, makes my sad point: or does it, for you, **what**? Can you believe that both sides can go on muddling with the one-track analysis without any suspicion that establishment economics, whether Marxist or Keynesian or post-either is, well, in my Dublin term, shite? I use the term because I was reminded of its psychic vigor recently by a story told in a recent interview by Liam Neeson. He had been performing in New York and went strolling in Central Park the next morning. He passed a stationary horse cab with the cabbie aloft. In a clear Dublin voice the cabbie remarked "Howaya Liam? I saw your play last night. It was shite!" For Liam, a joyful entertaining encounter. If you have come towards believing that there is a defect in both Team B's reading of the puzzle and Altman's standard reading, might you not make the same loud cheery claim? Might you not feel the urge to do something about it? There used to be an honorable Dublin trader titled a "nightshiteshifter": overnight he collected horse manure. We need a dayshiteshifter in New York.

What might we do about all this jetsam? Well, that is the puzzle of our beginning futurology. The previous chapter points both to the problem of interpreting simple economic facts and the problem of interpreting interpretation. Neither Team B nor the Establishment knows that the problem is one of pausing to think freshly and creatively, like Newton under the fabled apple tree. One wonders whether either group has ever really been pushed to serious interpreting, or are both sides, as the great Joan Robinson pointed out often, just brain-washed from Economics 101 on? I really will have to quote her later on that!

Meantime, I wish to add to your exercises. In chapter 5 I added the faulty diagrams that are embedded in the bad story of the past hundred years and more. Here I want to add a discussion and derivation of the correct diagrams that are to embed the good story of the next million years and more. They are to be followed up, in chapter 12 on doctrines, by an expression of the sane stand on money and profit that emerges from the understanding of the diagram. This sanity, the old man in Toronto told me in the autumn of 1977, will take 150 years to catch on. That leaves us 114 years to his forecast date. Maybe the futurology express will get us there by the end of this century?

There Are Two Types of Firm

Here I wish only to talk quite simply about how the working of any particular firm, as it is presented in any elementary economic text, is so simplified as to ground a fundamental disorientation of all of economic science and practice at all levels. This is an extraordinary claim, yet I would have you grasp it as your own claim. Already I have noted my own and your bent to push further. Will the simple fundamental adjustment to the beginning of economics that comes out of this small venture really lift economics towards a new seriousness that will cut out the idiot and selfish financial goings-on of places like Wall St., the stupidities of governments in their spending and tax-policies, international economic gangsterism, etc. etc.? As I noted at the beginning, the answers are in fact available. My challenge here is to make the silly mistake and the necessary new beginnings popularly evident through a few homely reflections and some associated diagrams. And all this is summed up in the slogan, mentioned at the beginning and given as title of this section: **there are two types of firms**. Taking that into account — **and** into accounting — leads to a science of economics that is to clean up all the mess of finances that have destroyed businesses and nations and cultures in the past one hundred years.

So, we start now with the standard diagram of current economic texts and move fairly smoothly to a diagram that points to that new science of economics that is to save us from global disaster. I wish you to come with me slowly and quietly from the standard diagram, through two transition diagrams, to the central scientific diagram of future economics.

We start with the standard Household to Firm diagram of the first weeks of elementary economics, with the obvious meanings for the symbols of Households, Firms, income, and demand:

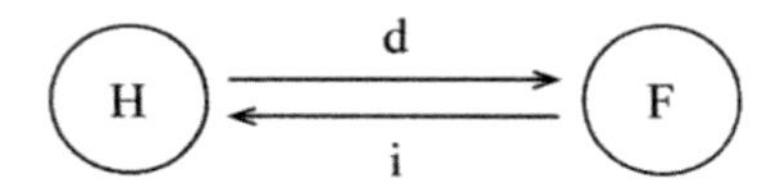

There is an easy way to add the second type of firm, which supplies not consumer goods, but stuff for the first type of firm: maintenance and innovative stuff, which I'll symbolize as mi. (Think of **m** as pointing to maintenance and more!! I am thinking of innovation of course.) Here you are:

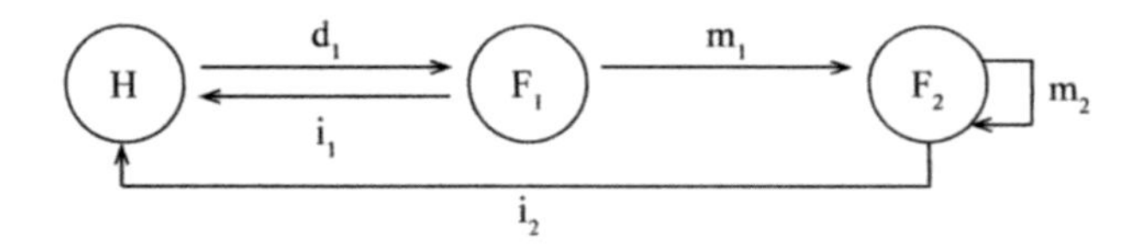

Notice now that F_2 is in the same boat as F_1 as regards maintenance and innovation. But we don't want to add F_3, F_4… I won't go into the simplification of packing in all the series of F_n into F_2.

I just claim here that it works empirically as grounding decent measurements of business flows.

But how do we get that into the diagram?

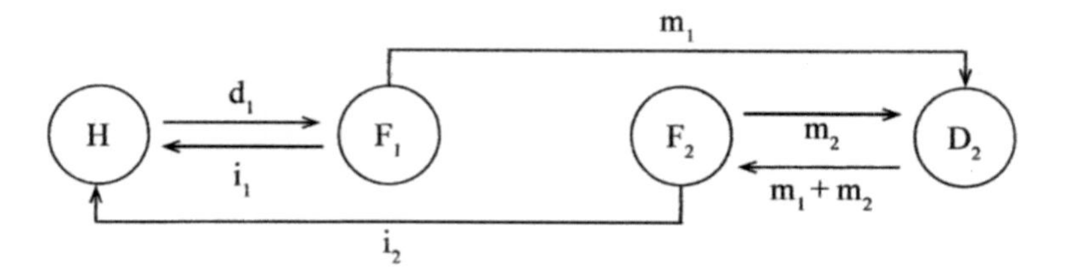

We can make this neater by thinking of two types of demand and, if you wish, replacing Households by D_1, with flow d_1 and making, e.g., d_2-type flowings from D_2, the demand of firms for capital stuff, marked in the diagram as m. Next, we find that we get a more workable diagram by laying the transactions out in a square and adding the flow lines:

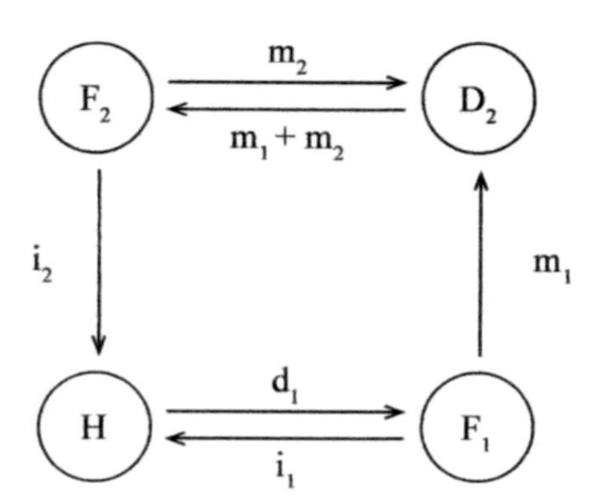

This would be the beginnings of a new economics of measurable flows, one that would yield norms of financing, of profit in both normal and innovative economies, etc. etc. But understanding THAT would be a slow climb through the efforts mentioned at the beginning. The fundamental need is to sort out this beginning before adding banks and taxes and international trading etc. etc.

CHAPTER 8
CRITICAL PAWS

Was Joan Robinson right on the ball in her steady criticism of the goings-on of economics in the past two centuries? Is McShane right regarding the drift away from the whatting of the *Upanishads* (*upa*: near; *ni*: devotedly; *shad:* sitting. I wish you sitting thus near *what*) that distances global loneliness from itself? These are issues of dialectic, of the group of elders that are pivotal in ever-freshening the foundational fantasy that is to save—stumblingly—our future skins. Here, thinking of Branson's Team B, we meet in fantasy the A-Team that grounds the Dream Team of the next specialized group. Do I have to caution you not to confuse these handy names with either television or criminal trials? Yet history and its entertainments are to be on trial here. Is Brazil really on the ball in building stadiums for world events when its population and its ecosystems are suffering such abuses? Was Joan Baez right to sing "what have they done to the rain?" Was Otto Klemperer more than joking when he mused that the good thing about contemporary classical music was that it was temporary? Was Eric Voegelin offensively erroneous to solemnly talk, in his wonderful English accent, of present academic structures as brothels of opinion? Was that eminence of Oxford, Gilbert Ryle, onto something when he glibly remarked to me that science was just stones rattling in a bucket? Finally, was Joseph Schumpeter ahead of the contemporary game when he claimed that "the banker's function is essentially a critical, checking, admonitory one"?

Am I not here all over the place and time of history? Yet the future A-Team has to be thus to fulfill its function, "essentially a critical, checking, admonitory one." The function is to have global reach of a character totally beyond the scope of Branson's B-Team. But I foresee troubled times in its first century, where its interest will coincide with that of the B-Team. Should we pause over that, or should we not rather reach out in fantasy in order to sniff the large task of these next millennia? So we reach in creative fantasy for the possibility and, with our whatting help, increasing probability of elders being spun up, by the previous groups, to being both on the present Global ball—like the first-class tennis player taking a brutal first serve—and venturesome in handling new twists of the big bang.

The problem of beginnings will occupy us in chapter 11 as a quiet and realistic personal problem and in chapter 15 as a realistically-challenging communal problem. In these present three chapters we reach for a vision of elders of a later time, seeking to build the house of history, yet paradoxically knowing that the house is to be an indefinite sky-scraper. As I type, there comes to mind my favorite quotation from Gaston Bachelard: "Late in life, with indomitable courage, we continue to say that we are going to do what we have not yet done: we are going to build a house." *The Poetics of Space* (Boston: Beacon Press, 1969), 61. I think of people like Nadia Boulanger and George Eliot, of whom I wrote already here. Both took their zones of interest with passionate seriousness. The future elders are to take all zones with passionate seriousness. Am I not then slipping into the old myth of the Renaissance man and woman, something now beyond us all? Indeed, not: I am weaving towards our way beyond the myth, beyond an elegant omni-competent sophistication that perhaps could be associated with Fontenelle (1657-1757), out into the fantasy of there being the communal support to generate this fourth group that dare to appreciate the world at and beyond the level of the times. Ortega y Gasset spoke thus of reaching the level of the times in *The Mission of the University*, but the A-Team that he spoke of in those lectures, that I write of here, would not be comfortable in present universities. Sadly, they would have been at home in Academus' garden, where Plato tried to do for the city something better than Lucky Luciano did for semi-organized crime.

But I would have you envisage these elders as they operate in the better world created by a millennium of cyclic futurology. There the ongoing task of dialectic is to have three regular clear layers, the first relatively private, the second radically private, the third brutally public. We take three chapters to fantasize about it, happy and contented as observers, "hurlers on the ditch," to use the Irish phrase for commentators who are generally negative and incompetent.

Our "checking, admonitory" commentators are to be powerfully positive. We pause first over their initial private positivity. And we need to add the fantasy that in another millennium things will be moving better, money will have the incarnate communal meaning of promise, dancing of words and limbs will brighten streets, and leisure, not employment, will be the bread of life.

The first task's set of activities involves a gathering of the cycle's present givings, new twists moving round, always selective, from research through interpretations and then through the story-tellers dealing with sub-tubes of the global doings or sometimes, like a new Toynbee, reaching out to the total past. But all this is within the full perspective of that later present Tower community. So there are assemblies, micro, meso, and macro, of recent pointers to progress. Each elder digests the novelties as well as the failures of old cycled suggestions and, as millennia pass, the whole process becomes more refined. The lifts of dance are to be assembled with increasing subtlety by subtle elders like, but so unlike, those on the related television shows, reacting in a manner that can be thought of as *Completion*, like the final joy of menu-musing. *Completion* is the let-loose reach of approval that may carry the elder into some ecstasy of welcome. It is an art critic who lets the art-work really get to alert bones and toned chemicals. And that "get to" is followed by the reflective connecting, affinely or opposedly, of related leaps in culture, be they in affine geometry or in delicate architectural oppositions. The reflective connecting, *Comparison*, flows into *Reduction* which indeed ferments from the effort to connect or group. Think of such grouping shifts in particle physics, and you will find that this helps in the struggle towards a meaning for *Comparison*. But not all leaps are basic paradigm shifts; some are richly cultural like an innovation in traditional Chinese dance forms. Such rich shifts are nudged aside towards later local doctrines of dance. What the elder seeks, *Selects*, is such shifts as are globally significant, positional pointers for humanity, like new depths of the re-discovery and sublation of the interpersonal promise that was originally money, that should never have been squeezed from its symbolic significance, that could carry humanity beyond finance in a nano-technic globe of ten billion half-acre gardens and ocean groves.

The important possession of the elder, a life-character, is the innovative flexibility of *Comparison*, like the flexibility of a great tennis player meeting the oddest of volleys. But perhaps we have said enough about *Comparison* when talking of vets and other detectors in chapter 2.

Such, in shocking brevity, is the solitary elder's challenge, sanely solitary in that, like Andrew Wiles struggling with Fermat's Last Theorem a decade ago, tuning into the relevant community eventually is needed, indeed earlier than Wiles allowed himself. But, quite apart from tuning into colleagues along the way there is a further deeper tuning-in to be done, a tuning to self, searching, like Bachelard—but beyond both Bachelard and Wiles—for the unfinished inner and outer house. "How am I poised in the cloudiness of my *moi intime* whose deepest openness reaches towards the skyscraper?" But let us save that for the musings of the next chapter.

What is important for you and me here is that, like good watchers at center court, we can muse over old standards that are and were always and will always be, and over emergent standards that are perhaps quite crazily beyond even our efforts at fantasy.

I am talking here of an assembly of the past that is selective and creative, even wildly so, but measured. Right through these three chapters we are musing about assembly with different meanings. But here I would have you strain creative fantasy to think of two assemblies that pirouette around molecular patterns and their meanings. So, I mention vertical assembly and what I would call linguistic assembly.

Both are huge topics and edge us forward to great hopes. We shall return to vertical assembly more fully in chapters 15 and 16 and to linguistic assembly in chapter 17. But here we are seeking a sense of the creative energy of critical paws, minds grasping for the flickers of subtle integral human goings-on.

First, then, there is the ongoing issue of vertical assembly. Each assembler here is exactly that: an ongoing issue of vertical assembly, a neuro-molecular complex issuing, mentally and linguistically, the results of the dance around *Comparison*. Is each assembler luminous about all this? : that a vertical assembly, spontaneously thought of as ***I*** and thus expressed in some language, is talking about self and other selves and other nouned complexes as hierarchically one, operatively assembled, as it were in stacks that begin below with components like neutrons and quarks and end above with trans-ape neuron sparks? Are we, critical paws, moving along, age by age, in self-assembling luminousness regarding these startling patterns, evolutionary throw-ups of vertical assemblies and self-assemblies? I suspect that you find this question very strange, yet it must be the underlying—but luminously so—mood of the searchers in this group. If little partial answers are reached then they are handed on to be cycled and recycled so that historians operating on the next round will have increased sensitivity regarding, e.g., the meaning of the Renaissance as a massive assembly of nouned realities that are vertically assembled, some indeed self-assembled in a hierarchy of refined ways. And indeed that the Renaissance has fame because of the abundance of nouned assemblies that not only show unity in time and space, but have an added virtuality that can be called *brilliance*.

Finally, there is the assembly that is implicitly spoken of, and obviously spoken in, in that first assembly. Nouning is surrounded by a family of—in any language—distinguished cousins. Are the distinctions merely descriptive? Might they be slowly sorted out trans-linguistically in their neuro-molecular and molecular verticalities, where molecular verticalities literally take on the formative fostering of local tongues by native hills? And of course the formative fostering of Helen Keller's paws, her replacement tongue, needs to be communally assembled in self-luminosity if all this searching is not to be betrayed at its roots by a brutal darkness blocking the essential.

Such are the hauntings that fantasy envisages as an ethos of critical paws, seeking to bring history forward in light and delight.

CHAPTER 9
PAWS POISED

The ethos of various assemblies talked of at the end of chapter 8 calls for, and caul, further solitary pausing and poising. Before reflecting on the content of that pause in Dialectic, I wish to note a convenient distinction that I make here, and a convenient strategy I introduce. There are two possible versions of the pause of which I write. There is the full pause of the person who is involved seriously in the cycle, or hopes to be involved in it. There is a lesser pause of one who wishes to know where they stand with regard to the challenge of collaboration. At this stage in your reading you may well be interested in the notion of a collaborative futurology without quite knowing where it leaves you, where you are realistically being invited to go. In that case, you may well find it better to brood over the content of chapter 11, which focuses on an elementary self-discovery that I would consider an essential part of future living: a new common sense that is to emerge. The beginnings of this new common sense are key to the cultural shift needed if we are to get out of the present illusions of economic non-science and work pseudo-ethics. You may well find your home in that common sense and still thus be effective in "rescuing futurology" in rescuing your own and other's future. Check your sense of your quest even now: you may feel that chapter 11 is closer to your present whatting. Here I take the high road. The pause is a pause of assessing the character of the elder that is to be at home in this part of the cycle.

The pause has to be honestly biographic and critical, yet hopeful. I have dealt with people of all ages in this matter and regularly refer to that old Beatles' song which talks of being needed and fed "when I'm sixty-four." One can battle one's way out of bad education at any age. And perhaps that battling is a good topic with which to start here.

What is the key battling? It is carrying the Childout Principle, or COPON, that I introduced earlier, into one's present leisured life. The leisure may require a courageous stepping aside. I was once asked by a professor of religion, in perhaps a moment of his illumination, what he might do with a free summer that was looming. My reply was that he might pause over some mathematical problems. He didn't of course. He goes ahead now in a usual way, sadly passing on rich but nominalistic comments on current authors regarding searchings in religion. Have I stirred you to some illuminated reaching? The reaching needed may require levels of gutsy withdrawal.

What is this carrying forward of, well, let us call it COPON, that I advocate? Its goal helps its identification: to discover in oneself the patterns of serious whatting. In more solemn terms, it is to find out for oneself what it is to do serious science, or to do science seriously. I mentioned just now levels of withdrawal. A key withdrawal is from a cultural notion of science that identifies it with careful detached observation in the context of some hypothesis. The science that I am talking about is a resonant appreciation of what one is stewing over, and the stewing, study, is just that, a relaxed heating up of one's incarnate **what**. That relaxed heating up of one's incarnate **what** may well have been crippled by a dozen years of schooling. For this reason my own efforts to rescue whatting regularly ramble away from school topics into the world of conundrums, puzzles, odd problem situations. So far, in this book, I would seem to have introduced only one puzzle: that dealing with the ups and downs of ABCDEF.... in chapter 6. But have I not introduced the puzzle that is the ups and downs of you, and indeed of the economy?

To that puzzling, about you and the economy, I return in chapters 11 and 12. Here I wish to turn you towards what might be called the higher ground of a decent grip of the type of understanding that is involved in mathematics and physics. Do I cause you to frown? Perhaps it's time to turn to chapter 11?

The higher ground I write of must be a shared grounding of those laboring in the Tower, and obviously of those laboring to critically improve the Tower. But here we face the realism of the various expertises of the elders in this functional specialty. There is to be a common solid competence in scientific understanding, one comfortable with the problematic of each advancing science, though not at home in the frontline work. Indeed, even within a particular discipline, or sub-discipline, being up with front-line work is not a realistic expectation. If you are reading along here, against the suggestion about turning to chapter 11, you will find that this question of competence throws you back to your school days, even to your days in university. Heavens, I think of conferences on quantum physics where some of those lecturing were not competent! And I think of a professor of general relativity I had to suffer under who had very little idea of the meaning of a tensor control of spacetime equations.

Think, now, of your education and puzzle with me over what you think is competence. It is certainly best detected in the ability to teach competently. Here typical illustrations of failure to teach and learn come to mind: defining a circle, getting square roots, finding the basis of the two forms of calculus, pushing forward towards a control of the meaning of Maxwell's equations. It would take me altogether too long to handle, in useful heuristic, such problems briefly here—you might try my freely-available website book, *Wealth of Self and Wealth of Nations*, chapter 3 for a start—but try now to express the definition of a circle. How does it come out, if it comes out at all? I recall asking an undergraduate class of forty students for this: only one in the group managed to get a half-answer out. By the end of the day, and more correctly by the end of the course, the group reached a horrified appreciation of how they had been victimized both in school and in the university. Briefly, if one is to understand one has to mess around at length and patiently, and one needs a teacher who appreciates this and, of course, appreciates the definitions that lurk behind words and techniques.

Notice now what I am doing here. I am talking as a struggling elder, struggling to imagine, or fantasize, later ages. I write as one who has tried this climb and taught in these various zones. I am showing forth the poise of my paws but including the further reaching of those paws, a reaching that is deemed by me to be part of the genetic effort of us all if we are to understand and remedy this mess. So, you see a duplication: I am teaching about the handling of the mess in a way that looks to telling both of its bases—the basis of the mess **and** the telling—and of the developments that would occur beyond the mess.

So "Paws Poised" as a project for you and me can be thought about in terms of an extended autobiography, one extended into our own and the global future.

This is what one ends up passing on to one's checkmates. Have I done the extended autobiography in this book? Well, we are just nearing the halfway mark. Besides, my biographic ramble has been deliberatively incomplete. Still, you can get a sniff of it from that crazy website of mine. We can share the further ramble, a foundational ramble, by musing through the rest of this book, perhaps startling you as I ramble oddly, at the end of chapter 20, to my posthumous autobiography.

But meantime, I pause over my message here, a futurology expression that rises from a horrifying luminosity about the past of our hungers and cruelties, our education and economics, even our intertwined religions—I have strategically avoided that zone of our lives so far. The objective horror has all tumbled forward in what is almost entirely technological competence, without understanding or self-understanding. We have been taking square-roots uncomprehendingly yet so efficiently for millennia:

but what if we really needed cube-roots? We do not understand how to take any roots, much less how to root about in that failure.

I have rambled here very loosely to nudge you towards a sense of the existential challenge of a life-review that identifies the existential gaps. I have not ventured into the details of such gaps, and it has been a problem for me: what more to talk about in this chapter. An earlier venture of mine about the biography of climbing helps sense the broad difficult climb: *Cantower* 9 of my Website *Cantower* series. The emphasis there is on the key climbing needed within and beyond traditional philosophy. Also a return now to musing over the two diagrams that I placed at the end of chapter three obviously would help. My ramble raises the question of the exercise of these elements of you in the full range of inquires that the elder must mesh into a view on the front-edge of the level of the times. But I will say no more about this discomforting challenge until we get to chapter 18.

Meantime, I return to the "problem for me: what more to talk about in this chapter." Might we pick up on the mood of the third chapter? Then we hold our focus on whatting, what, what-more. The elder has to live in the discomfort of all aspects of these what-mores, and that discomfort will be brought to fuller subtlety as we weave together towards and in the final chapter of this little book. But its full ongoing turn-around can be spoken of here in broad terms relevant both to the future elders and to you now, whether or not you are hoping to take the high road or to move on a lower effective plane of meaning.

The issue is the personal cultivation of what is called *authentic nescience*. It is an issue which haunts this book and so haunts feebly the turns and types of words and phrases used. Think of "the tadpole of history." But think for how long and with what longing? We are back with the question raised just now about autobiography. We are back at re-reading the book of ourselves within the few pages above. We are forward to puzzling about the meaning of ***question raised.*** I recall now a slogan of mine that dominated a course I used to teach called "The Child as Quest." The slogan was "when you are raising children you are raising questions."

Were you raised by my ramble about your life-story? What is it to raise a question about a life, my life, of stumbling battered whatting? There is a tadpole-quest for the tadpole and the unknown frog of history and of my story. The unknown of my story, like that of the sick pup, has shadows cast on it by previous battered achievements, some of them glorious like Beethoven or Boulanger. But the tadpole of history is not frog-shadowed. Towards that absence our whatting should reach out in longing galactic loneliness, but our culture, its pundits and politicians, would laugh at such a reach, and cross the pub floor to the everyday bar with modest familiarity. "Whatilya have?" "The usual." We are ever invited to come out of the British Museum, as C.S. Lewis's devil would have it, and cherish the red double-decker bus, the real London that is now and ever shall be.

The final piece of this second of the tasks of dialectic is to step beyond the usual, the pseudo-permanence of the tadpole's muddling swim. It is to do the Nijinsky leap of *The Spectre of the Rose* right out of the window of today's light and its dark pint. The elder's last fling, before meeting checkmates, is to spell out in crippled luminousness, ability-best, both the what-norms of the heart and the frail fantasy of the unknown frog. So, each prepares, with relentless devotion, to try to add some increment to, or occasionally to leap quite beyond, the present standard model.

I risk, in conclusion, quoting the end of another chapter nine here, a risk indeed of teasingly giving my game away. It is the end of the ninth chapter of a little book by Bernard Lonergan called *Insight*.

"All we know is somehow with us; it is present and operative within our knowledge; but it lurks behind the scenes, and it reveals itself only in the exactitude with which each minor increment to our knowing is effected. The business of the human mind in this life seems to be, not contemplation of what we know, but relentless devotion to the task of adding increments to a merely habitual knowledge."

CHAPTER 10
CHECKMATES

Obviously here we have another layering of the process of assembling. But I would note that it is an assembling of mates. The elder has checked the new pointings in the sense of checking them in, with, and into the prior common worldview, shared Standard Model, of those in cyclic collaboration. But is it really a common view? Yes, with normal allowances for personality and language deviations. You may remember the mention of Chinese dance patterns in chapter 8 and extend now your thinking to words as local patterns and cranial neurochemistry as culturally patterned. In that first part of the dialectic process such differences are set aside in one's dynamic searching and are later swung back into circulation in, e.g., the final two specialties.

Obviously the mates in the checking dialogue do not, in actual dialogue, set aside, e.g., their quaint ways of talking and gesturing. But they are luminous about their positionings and poisitionings—a tricky distinction there that is talked of in *Cantower* 9 mentioned in my chapter 9—and now are serious and open about the possible fundamental shifts that may well be either shrunken or enhanced by local and personal culture.

One may well think of the assembling at this stage as a gathering of elders, but, to be effective, the gathering requires the articulation by each mentioned at the end of the previous chapter, in shared languages and symbols—and to the problem of translinguistic symbols we return all too briefly in chapters 16, 17, and 18. Then there is seen to emerge textual help to the matey checking: what is omitted in different assemblies, and how completion, comparison, reduction, classification, selection, show variations across the group. The variations are most often not fundamental, but occasionally one elder adds a new twist, like Feynman with his famous Feynman diagrams. I would note here a small but important point. I have mentioned Feynman diagrams just as I might mention Waddington's genetic drawings, but the occurrence of names in this context has generally nothing intrinsic to do with opinions. Maxwell's equations have a name attached to them for convenience. The science of humans is a space-time spread helped by such identifications. Botany is full of such naming: the *William Shakespeare 2000* rose by any other name would smell as sweet.

We need here to think and fantasize concretely about this communal effort of assembly, using analogies from successful sciences. The assembling is more and more a virtual-media business. There is the history of journals, but now they are increasingly e-journals. The pace of checking is a thing of globally-clocked exchanges. The push most of the time is for refinements of concrete determinations, actual occurrences, of standard model content, including positive suggestions regarding the shifting statistics of their occurrence. The group may refine the concrete characterization of some village contribution to progress, but it could also take account of present distributions of such village contributions. Such refining and accounting have then to be weaved into the foundational perspective of the consenting mates so as to be elegantly batoned on, batted on, to the next group of specialists, those who are committed to foundational fantasy, its maintained average velocity, and its particulate accelerations.

All this is impossibly general for a beginner, a first reader here, to get a grip on. A later cycle through the entire little book will help and I make the point here because I would have you note that there is the possibility of a beginner doing this section's task well, in an initial way, and in a commonsense fashion, by finding mates at the same level of checking. So, one may assemble stuff from this little book, and follow through the other sub-task of chapter 8 as best one can, tuning to one's own perspective and its projections in the pattern of chapter 9. Then one's mate or mates, doing the same, can be expected to bring one to a better tuning. The mates, of course, are mates who have read the book with some sense of its plausibility and some commitment to its larger view of progress. One does not really benefit from expressing sections of the book—any book—to or at a hostile acquaintance. That sort of expression and counter-expression is perhaps recreational for some, but it is dysfunctional.

I have some more scientific pointers on this that will be the core of chapter 17 below, but here I simply muse over the question that may have occurred to you here, or at any stage in your reading. "Would it not be better to include all types of checkmates in these goings-on, or indeed in any of the suggested goings-on of the book?" You already have my answer in the final sentence of the previous paragraph. The fuller answer pivots on complexities talked of in chapters 16, 17, and 18, but let us pause over the question through popular paralleling with scientific progress. Take, then, physics. I could start with the physics of the planet and humorously note that members of the flat-earth society do not participate in geophysical or astronomical conferences. But move to levels of sophistication and think of an entrenched Newtonian attending a conference on either relativity theory or present quantum theory. Work your way through other sciences and check—yes, mate, check!—for parallels. I do not do that here because the paralleling becomes weaker as we climb up through the more difficult sciences. Why? Well, that is a tricky question that needs the adventures of our thinking our way through these next chapters to refinements of pointers regarding futurology as dialectic.

My key point here is the optimistic one that futurology is to move closer in its standards to those of physics as it moves from seed to science in these next centuries. But note now, very helpfully I think, that physics has to, needs to, move into and with futurology if it is to shake off present muddles. The muddles are in physics, the philosophy of physics, the technologies of physics, the educative dynamics of physics, and popular talk and thought of physics: altogether too much for the corner of a chapter. But let us just muse vaguely over the question, What is physics? My vague answer is that physics is the simplest science, dealing with the most elementary parts of our vertically-assembled cosmos. It is, normatively, a cyclic science as is any other zone of human inquiry. Curiously, the cyclic problem has emerged in the more difficult and less mature sciences, such as the science of literature, but it is nonetheless increasingly manifest in physics' need to tune into its history and to take stock of its future eco-impact.

Here, in my reference to the past and future of physics, you may suspect yet another structure of assembly that is relevant, especially in that zone of omnidisciplinary mates. Your suspicion may reflect the contemporary tunnel-vision of specializations, where, even in physics only the best hold it all together—recall Feynman's famous three-volume *Lectures in Physics* of the early 1960s. But the question may also have arisen in the present context of mates from different disciplines checking on progress.

The cyclic answer to the problem is had in acknowledging an assembly that I have named ***sloping***. If you are thinking of the eight collaborative groups with an image of "four going up and four going down," then we can split our reflections on sloping into two, and indeed that is what I do in this little book. The sloping down, quite different from the up-sloping, is something I deal with in chapter 14. What, then, of the sloping up that solves, pragmatically, the problem of the isolation of disciplines and interests? The elementary diagramming of the sloping is, as we'll quickly see, not difficult. Think of the apparently-isolated reality of an investigated object: a physics-reaction recorded, a butterfly pinned down, a scroll found at the Dead Sea. The solitariness of focused isolation of the discovery yields in the cycle to a convergence of disciplines: there is a shared computered record in the laboratory, there is the pin for the butterfly, there is carbon-dating for the scroll. Further convergence occurs when one moves to the story either of the find or of its discovery. There is nothing at all abstract about history, and it is for that reason that facts are the haunt and hunting ground of history. You may muse further on a panoply of instances of such slopings and gradually attempt a useful diagram. It might be like a series of possible house-roofs angling up from separate points at angles between, say, 10° to 80°. How to order the disciplines? That depends on convenience and discipline, but eventually the mates need some consensus regarding symbolizations, or rather, regarding sophistications of symbolizations: for we are trying to fantasize the goings-on of a mature futurology.

But let us take a simpler tack on the mates working together. First I give a nudge towards context, which should haunt the simple collaborative story that is to follow. The nudge in bold face, to get enlarged on in chapter 18, is the sentence that begins the next paragraph.

There is, no doubt, to be a great lift towards conversations meshed in subtle symbolizations. To help you imagine this type of conversation think of, go to the library and check, the incomprehensible flow of topic and symbols in, say, the *Journal of Symbolic Logic*. Do I hear you exclaim, "But surely this is not necessary!"? Why would you thus exclaim? Such questioning pushes us both back to a fuller musing on the boldfaced statement. You note then my seriousness: it is a doctrinal—really, a metadoctrinal—claim of mine. It may need systematic contextualization, such that particular systems are invoked and local possibilities considered. We get into our own little puttering with the forward specialties to sniff out the futurological seeds or weeds in my claim.

Would it not be better if I, an Elder mate, were better prepared for conversation regarding that boldfaced claim? Would it not, indeed, be better if I wrote out the surrounds of my metadoctrine?

So we come to a simple tack on the mates working together. They would improve their futurological effort considerably if they, so to speak, **booked** their latest push or refinement. Well, yes, think of each of the mates as writing such a book, not a compacting of the standard model, but their push, like Higgs presenting a paper on that famous particle. Think, then, of perhaps ten leading mates making their books available to one another. The ten mates have now ten books to brood over—their own, of course, is included. How do they read these books? It needs to be done in the manner of a fresh start: back then to the suggestions made, or lurking subtly, in chapters 8 and 9, back to the climb from this assembly of ten volumes through the other facets of the struggle.

This is surely tough work beyond the call of duty?

It is the call, and they are the caul, of a duty both to the future and to their own lonely **whats**.

What, **what**, is to be handed on to the community of the fifth specialty is a hard-won consensus. That foundational community—or think of it as each individual in the community—is facing forward and pacing forward, like a runner with hand out behind for the baton, trustingly. The collaboration pivots on cyclic trust. The tadpole strains to cross the frog-line.

So, there emerges a lift in the standard model, a lift that could be identified as a lift from history's struggling messy operating norms to a genetic grip on its best, and so regularly neglected, fruitful frogmeantary ideas. So, through the best effort of the present best, there emerges what might be called an idealized version of previous reaches of humanity, showing the past as better than it was.

Chapter 11
Foundations: I Am What

From various previous chapters I have referred forward to this chapter as one in which you can get an elementary grip on your own positive perspective on futurology. Are you crazy enough to aim for collaboration in seeding the Tower, or should you find a lesser way? The great thing about the lesser positive way is that it too seeds the functional collaboration of the Tower.

Forget the higher way for the moment and just focus on the reaching for a commonsense appreciation of two concrete related features of the foundations of futurology that have been floating about in the text from the beginning. These two features I number now (10) and (11). The numbers are of no consequence here: I return to the question of their choice in the Epilogue. (10) refers to the mess in modern culture that begs for the collaboration that I name futurology; (11) is the component in that mess that is the heart of our politico-economic shambles. The rest of the flotsam and jetsam of this little book can be named (1) through (9), and we attend to that in more detail in the later chapters. So, I am talking, throughout the book, of a self-identification, a self-luminous identification, that is to mature into spinning foundations for the entire cycle. Spinning foundations? I mean of course the people, who are the foundations of the entire cycling.

Here I would have you express—perhaps in both senses!—your own futurology in relation to (10) and (11). It is a task that is obviously a piece of the task described in chapter 9 but away from the world of checkmates in chapter 10. It is a matter of musing privately and with some decent degree of honesty—it is not that easy, as we all know, to be honest with one's *moi intime*!—about where you stand with regard to (10), functional collaboration as a vital piece of future progress, and with regard to (11), how you might talk about the basic mess of economics. Note that the first search is not for action but for your position right now on the basic push of this book: for the division of labor that underlies the cyclic care of progress. The second search is a discerning of expected habits of talk about the economy and its organization.

Your stand on (10) obviously can result in talk, but the core is a Yes or a No. It is to be a modest yes or no, a nodding or naying to the persuasiveness of what I presented. Think of it as a viewing of a menu outside a restaurant, to see what looks good or even preferable. You are not seriously concerned about going to eat there. I won't go on to describe the entrée on the menu or the process of climbing to a choice. We have been musing on that, on the maître d', on the chefs, on the décor, the music and dancing, etc., right through. There is the dish and decor that I point to, a future hope rather than a present achievement: think of those TV shows where the retired soccer-player, Ramsey, uses strong language to recommend change. Then there is a group of entrées, a list of those that point out new structures, Samaritans without borders or whatever. A leading group of these, in relation to economics, is Branson's B-Team. Then there are all the other entrées which we lump together as somewhat fixed in the status quo of varieties of capitalism and communism backed by present global muddled education and banking. The present pause is an is-pause, but I would have you do it in the COPON mood. Figure out, a tricky task, whether it is an is-question, or an is-to-do question, and then whether it is a for-someone-else-to-do is-to-do-question. That figuring weaves into the what-questioning and answering that is an ongoing growth in self-understanding. That, as you remember, is the heart of the COPON principle which regards to how you are to teach children, but now in fact can be seen as applying to self-teaching. The COPON principle, recall, is "when teaching children geometry one is teaching children children." The broader principle is "when reaching to understand anything, reach to understand yourself, and when reaching to understand yourself, reach to understand something." It is an aim, even in common sense, to be clear to yourself about your doings.

So, here, the issue—literally—is to be a what-answer to "What am I when I am puzzling?" and you should now add what am I doing when I talked about my puzzle, the puzzle that is me, the puzzle that is progress.

My suggested answers (10) and (11) in this book are bookmarks in the puzzling. I would wish you to move forward with a luminous active view on these two zones. What I insist on here is that that luminous active view does not demand that you go beyond normal commonsense meaning. Think, for instance, of a friend's reaction to something you say: "do you hear yourself? Have you lost your mind?" Well, you may not have lost your mind, but you need to find your mind.

I write of the issue twistedly: something is to issue in you. What is the issue, the mind-body stance, to be? It is to be a break with present victimization. There is a sense in which the stirrings all over the globe, occupying Wall Streets or various Squares, are an expression of victimization and the need to break from it. Yet the stirrings are massively sick with victimization. We have been truncated, left headless, by accepted patterns of behavior in education, economics, and endeavors of a five-day week, and these patterns weave into our protests. The deeper issue, then, is the effort to find our minds and our cherished mindings, and to grow towards taking a stand on what is needed in our selves and in our times for that finding. So we are back with the messed-up family of chapter one and the title of chapter four, "What Rescues Futurology" with or without a question mark. What rescues futurology? What rescues futurology. What rescues the future? Futurology is to rescue the future, futurology is to rescue **what**.

Futurology is to rescue your what, here and now. THAT is our midway pause, our chapter 11 identification: facing bankruptcy and flaking, peeling, it off in an inner fashion. So, we are to arrive at "Expressing Futurology" and a rescuing of "What Are We." Have we not neatly got ourselves back to the wall, and started a fresh turn-around? "What I am" is to be expressed—double meaning here!—in a new way. Indeed! "**What** I am" and it has been stolen from me. It has been stolen from me by institutions that have taken corrupt shape through millennia of structured pretensions and greed. But I can take a first step for myself—indeed, for my children and friends too, in my fermenting their COPON—by rescuing the What in me, perhaps even here now in my chapter 11 bankruptcy. But that first step, in my invitation, is to cognize—not recognize, for recognition is a recovery and our whats have been brutally covered all our lives—that the institutions of corruption cannot be expected to move towards a liberation that would make them extinct. There is needed some strange large other loose type of institution to storm und drum these monsters off our streets, our globe. Have you a better suggestion than the one I have made here: the seeding, shooting, and shaping of a community collaborating in global care?

There you have my question for you regarding (10), a question incompletely posed in this halfway chapter. Think your way round the other options. Especially think your way round about that option that is victimhood in its saddest expression: "What is the government going to do about X?" An accumulation of victims in a square or at a wall or round a summit merely binds the victims together, perhaps even in psychic contagions, and shifts the institutions to new devices of victimization and indeed, self-victimization.

But enough said now to contextualize my suggestion (10) as a halfway house: we have ten more stories. And to introduce our next story is, in our turn around, to get our paws on, as I wrote above, "(11), the component in that mess that is the heart of our politico-economic shambles."

Getting your paws on this requires that you take seriously—as seriously as a good class in physics or good economics (which does not exist yet!)—my pedagogical invitation here, which carries forward from the end of chapters 5 and 7. In a good physics class we would only occasionally and casually take in what parallels the stuff referred to the end of chapter 5: the errors or bad theories of past physics. But you could usefully putter around with the defective diagrams there, perhaps find that you really cannot break out from the mentality expressed in the diagrams. Always, one is battling the present culture of simple answers "taken in" nominally, whether they are correct or erroneous.

So my invitation here is to your battling to ingest and express the sane position expressed at the end of chapter 7.

Are you up for that battle here and now? It is to be, like Newton, a matter of days or weeks, soaking up the concrete flow of real business. This is, has been, the stumbling block for members of the economic community. Amazingly, they are deeply closed to simple creative thinking. My heroine of economics, Joan Robinson, kept pointing this out through her life. There is the hilarious report of her reading Keynes' manuscript of *The General Theory*, telling him that she found a certain area obscure: Keynes, in reply, admitting that he did too. Keynes' *General Theory* was nicely simplified a year after publication by John Hicks, who gave us the nonsense of the IS/LM curve that has dominated thinking since.

But let us not get into that miserable story here. Rather, let us be warned by Joan Robinson's view of the education of economists. Don't get hung up on the details, which relate to the mess of measuring capital. Focus rather on the mood of modeling and of the end product of the whole cover-up.

> The student of economic theory is taught to write $O = f(L, C)$ where L is a quantity of labor, C a quantity of capital and O a rate of output of commodities. He is instructed to assume all workers alike, and to measure L

in man-hours of labour; he is told something about the index-number problem involved in choosing a unit of output; and then he is hurried on to the next question, in the hope that he will forget to ask in what units C is measured. Before ever he does ask, he has become a professor, and so sloppy habits are handed on from one generation to the next.

"The Production Function and the Theory of Capital," *The Review of Economic Studies*, vol. 21, no. 2 (1953-54), 81-106, at 81.

I would have you take in a giant foundational point here about the cultured passivity in classrooms—and in the larger class-grooms of TV and politics—a passivity that dominates our lives from kindergarten to senior days. But the problem is the cultivation of a "take in" which cannot be a take-in in the same old cultural passivity. We are back with the nudges of the beginning of the book, nudges that realistically you cannot take seriously till you finish a first read and then: then, take a stand about this invitation to take a stand around, within, (11). In that manner you may stay with me and settle, impossibly, for a few Newtonian weeks of scrambling to escape the brainwashing of economic teachings and daily loud-mouthings regarding Stock exchanges and interest rates.

If you are to stay with me and be, existentially, within a sane perspective on the nonsense of our politicians and bankers, then you must anticipate some strange days of puttering imaginatively about, perhaps, little local businesses. No silly escape into modeling C, L, O. I once lectured in a small city of India on the topic of two types of firms, and we focused on a familiar sight on the streets: side-walk barbers armed with a chair and some simple equipment like old-style clippers backed by comb and scissors. The comb, the clippers, the chair are not everlasting assets. What happens when one of them fails? How, then, do the rupees flow? If the barber is using up the meager income every week, what does he or she do—I never saw a she there—when the comb breaks? So you may thus, on your own town's streets, notice two flows and slowly find that the diagram which concludes chapter 7 makes sense. Then you can go back and find what is missing in the diagrams at the end of chapter 5.

When you muse over the comb or the diagrams in chapter 5, you will begin to note a missing flow or set of flows in that concluding diagram of chapter 7. You might even have a shot at fitting suitable flows in. Then, indeed, you will have had a Newtonian week or year! But you would still have a decent distance to go to sort out the mess of *C*, *L*, *O* and the concrete rhythms that are the full set of flows. That would be like the intellectual distance between Newton and Laplace.

CHAPTER 12
ECONOMIC DOCTRINES

Enough, for the moment, on the invitation to take a stand on that concluding diagram of chapter 7. In chapter 16 we return to the general issue of taking a stand on diagrams, diagrams that help us to hold together the subsets (1) to (9) that I mentioned in the last section. Here I wish you—even if you did not pause for a week or a year over the ends of chapter 5 and 7!—to get some impression of the valid doctrine of profit that eventually will replace the ungrounded doctrine that is blindly and greedily accepted at present.

We are here skimming through the zone of the sixth functional specialty, FS_6. If we were seriously in that zone, then we would be moving mindfully in a style, a context, quite remote from commonsense chat about profit. This is not something that is easy for untutored common sense to ingest, and unfortunately that is the common sense bred in most of our schools and even in our universities. There you regularly get a formula or a richly informed, even aesthetically apprehended, presentation of the result of someone's previous thinking or their delusions. Exams require a commitment to short term memory, but as Joan Robinson notes, usage can fix it in long-term memory without any transition to comprehension. Let us leave that aside now and do some creative skimming.

We could start with the Indian barber, or—as I do in other writings—with my own family's little bakery business in the Dublin of the 1940s. But here, in our hurry, I move to a broader situation beyond capital equipment's irreparable breakdown—a comb breaks, a van-horse dies—and there is creative innovation. I stay here with a realistic instance, and I introduce the correct notion of credit. The correct notion is neatly conveyed by adverting to a usual Irish statement regarding, say, some achievement: "you have to give her credit for that." You do know pretty well what that means. But push it now in regard to my favorite illustration of economic innovation: the lady in the story has the achievement of inventing the shift from spade-spud culture to horse-plough culture. You, of course, may have better illustrations, or wish to go large scale to consider trains or airplanes. But stay with my Irish island of primitive times: further leads will be given in the Epilogue. Indeed, a key set of leads is given immediately, in that it is best that I complete the final diagram of chapter 7 now, and I do so by stealing it from page 92 of my little book, *Economics for Everyone: Das Jus Kapital* (Halifax: Axial Publishing, 1998). Further, I see no sense in modifying its odd namings. The main pointing is towards you taking serious note of the addition of a central zone.

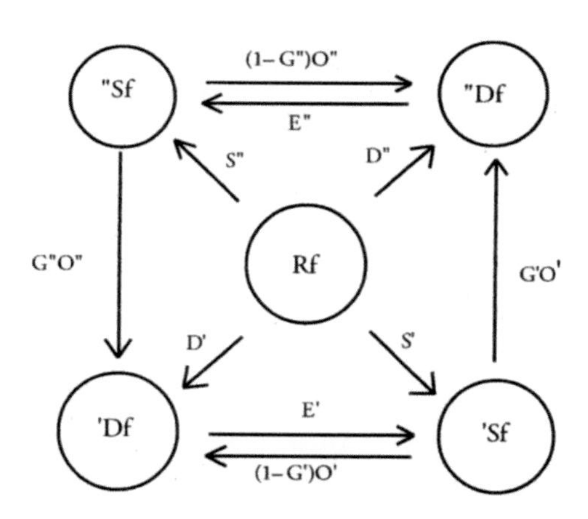

The diagram allows you to go back now to the erroneous diagrams at the end of chapter 5, but that certainly takes patient work beyond my simple doctrinal text. Meantime, some light on the complex diagram. I have revised the names in the circles and, of course, added the key central circle, but I have not changed the diagram. The revision brings us from pedagogy of the prior diagram to a beginning of system, a standard move into serious understanding. But the central circle is what merits your immediate attention. Think of it as a circle involving the holding and inventing of money, and go back, as you struggle, to musing on the faulty standard diagrams that I added at the end of chapter 5.

Think of it, thus? There is a brilliant move there equivalent to a leaping of Isaac Newton in physics: you get the holding and inventing of money out of the direct flow of economic goings-on.

Forget, for the moment, the exchanges of money that relate to changes of ownership like selling or buying a second-hand house or factory, or a share of a business. And certainly let us not get derailed into the crazy area of selling, sharing, shuffling, debts. That is a complex mess that accelerated massively in the past fifty years.

So, on we go with our doctrinal focus. We are interested in profit, as a piece of economic structure. Doctrinal presentations normally slip past refinements, be they systematic or concrete. The slipping past has various grounds. First there is the slipping past that occurs in the cyclic collaboration. Foundational persons pick up on new twists of strategy or better twists on an old failed strategy and go on to nudge the doctrinal community to bring the new doctrine into doctrinal focus: where might it fit in the structured doctrines of the zone? The new doctrine, in that case, will have neither a decent systematic content nor the additions of concrete reference. All along here we are talking—but so vaguely!—of seriously understood doctrines that are quite remote from what I may call street doctrines. Am I writing here about such a new doctrine? I must distinguish now, in a distinction that should help you to understand the cyclic collaboration better.

Yes, I am writing about a new doctrine within FS_6; but it has been developed within a complex scientific viewpoint that leaps forward from the analysis around the diagrams at the end of chapter 7, with the addition of this new five-circle diagram. That new doctrine can be stated within the small core of that essential slice of a system. It can be illustrated within that slice, and indeed has been. But it lacks the fullness that it will have when it is twined into the ongoing genetics—mostly, here a transformed criticism of ill-treatments—of the sick puppy that is actual economics. Actual economic theory at the moment, as tossed around by these pre-scientists, is like the early days when malaria was associated with bad air. Not altogether early days, of course: that was the bad air of thinking about bad air as the cause of the London cholera in the 1850s when Dr. John Snow was pushing the establishment for a serious shift of viewpoint and the engineer Joseph Bazalgette was pushing, against the great stink of London, towards the re-building of its sewers.

Present economic theory and behavior stinks. What is wrong? Well, you can think of bad air or London sewers or the atmosphere in Wall Street or the solemn air of Economics 101. At all events, I had best now state the doctrine in FS_6, a doctrine which has available backing from a slice of FS_7, but obviously no scientifically-elaborated FS_8, much less concrete illustrations relevant to the persuasiveness needed in C_9. The doctrinal statement is the following paragraph.

Profits are of two kinds. There is ordinary profit that is required in order to ensure maintenance of the economic enterprise. Then there is the profit that can enable the implementation of an innovative idea within the business. The latter profit may not be available in coincidence with, concomitant to, the new idea, in which case there is the financial facility of credit. That facility, in the presence of a new idea, is regularly creative of what is called money.

There you have it, in 80 words. I suspect that the doctrinal shifts in physics of Einstein or Schrödinger or Higgs could be stated in less words. Or one might think of statements of doctrinal shifts in psychology made by Karen Horney or statement by Schoenberg of twelve-tone shifts in classical composition. But such statements are made in a relatively mature sciences or techniques, where refined jumps are slowly admitted. This economic doctrinal statement, however, is made in a culture of deeply-rooted conventions of a non-science, where refined jumps can only be admitted in usual patterns of statistical cover-ups. The statement would be, is indeed, taken up in that context.

The difficulty is that the statement has to be taken up within its own minimal systematic context and this is something that disputants simply refuse to do. What about the openness of your what in this back-to-the wall situation? I wrote of innovation needing profit of a distinct type, profit beyond maintenance. Suppose it is not available: then financing would have to come from the fifth circle. What your *what* has to do is detect the shifts in the set of flows that occur. Recall now our ABC puzzle of chapter 6. Genuine detecting requires a patient openness if one is to leap to the hidden rule, the new law of rhythms.

Now the law in fact is not new: it is embedded in the rhythms of economics and indeed evident enough to have been noticed by bright people in the past two hundred years: there are great names associated with that hunt. Their detecting was successful only in establishing more complex economic facts that are insufficiently distinguished. Think of the work of Marx or the two big volumes on *Business Cycles* of Schumpeter published, unfortunately, in 1939, when the Second World War offered a handy cover-up. And of course there was the New Deal, tying in nicely with Keynes and Hicks. Alvin Hansen addressed the American Economic Association at the time and noted that business cycle theory was a thing of the past.

The difficultly of adequately detecting here is that the needed detecting belongs to a new systematics based on the minimal system surrounding the new doctrine. That detecting is of the sort that can work through a history of the sickness of the puppy that is economics so that the battle of the inner genetics against the twisted patterns of the disease can be not only sophisticatedly revealed but also reversed to become complex positive elements in a larger genetic systematics.

You are somewhat lost here, are you not? That is because the 80 words of the immediately previous paragraph are metadoctrinal.

To enter doctrinally into a changed perspective in a cycle requires a focus on the systematic surround of a doctrinal change. That doctrinal change, with its systematic surround, can be so disruptive as to be a paradigm shift that shakes up the full geohistorical genetic sequencing. Such shifting is most evident in the creative chemistry of Lavoisier or of Mendeleev. It goes deeper here in economics in that the shift equivalent to a shift in economics is like the shift from alchemy to chemistry.

How is the paradigm barrier to be broken? The full shift takes place when the cyclic collaboration spirals the doctrine through the entire global cultural system and the various statistics of its presence shift in general to the patterns of normal law curves. That may take a century or more. Meantime the barrier to be broken needs luck and a focus of crisis, like the Michelson-Morley experiment in physics. The experiment in economics that has failed brutally and unhumanly, because of its grounding in ignorance and greed, is the experiment that sacrifices the central functional of economic life to the gaming, with the central circle, of neurotic financiers. To the problem of creating destructive luck in this madness we return in the concluding sections of chapter 14.

CHAPTER 13
GLIMPSING THE SYSTEMATICS OF FUTUROLOGY

In the previous chapter, where the focus was on the sixth specialty of the collaborative cycle, I met the challenge of intimating the nature of doctrines at that stage of the Tower cycle by risking a doctrinal statement of fundamental economic doctrines. The presentation was pretty incomprehensible to you at the level at which it is meant in that specialty, thus illustrating very bluntly the character of Tower work. Am I here to try something similar, a dense systematics of Futurology? That is a hopeless task. Yes, I could start off with a pretty exact definition, nominal to many of my readers, meaningful and even startling to those familiar with my previous work. Here it is: "Futurology is the conception, affirmation, and implementation of the integral heuristic structure of future historical being." The key aspect of it in this chapter is the conception; in the next chapter the focus is on implementation. The issue here is the style of the conception, and my effort here is to give some pointers to that style.

I look back on my own struggling to get to grips with the systematics relevant to the future and keenly sympathize with fresh searchers in this task. When one thinks of system against the background of normal western education and culture, one tends of think of Euclid on the one hand, and systems that are mechanical or thermodynamic on the other. Euclid builds his system from basic propositions that are called axioms: one finds the same approach in such diverse chaps as Archimedes, Thomas Aquinas, and Newton.

I have already invited a stretching beyond that type of structure by introducing the problem of the sick or healthy puppy. Is there an axiomatics of the pup? One might make a case for claiming yes for, so to speak, a cross-section of the life of a puppy, but it has weaknesses related to the strange hierarchic structure that we talked about in chapter 8. Suppose it done, though: then you might imagine the healthy pup heading for doghood as a sequence of ordered axiom systems: forget, for the present, both sicknesses and death. The question that now emerges is about the order: what sort of order is it? It is a uni-directional order, but odd in that it is what Schrödinger talked about in the 1950s, in Trinity College Dublin, as **negentropic**. It goes against the thermodynamic grain. It is somehow an intussusception and infolding of energy. Here I wish to dodge debates about the nature of energy: its real meaning is, curiously, quite the opposite of our normal usage of the word, relating not to outburst potential but to infolding possibilities. But at all events we are now thinking of a type of systemization in the pup or the flower that is unlike mathematical system in that it involves axiom-structures that are, so to speak, concretely on the move, and it is unlike the systems of physics or chemistry in that the motion is ordered against the entropy that governs these two zones. The further unlikeness to physical and chemical systems was already slipped into our musings in that none of us ever seriously talk about a sick chemical system: although serious Irish Guinness drinkers might use such words in regard to a bad pint!

Moving on from there, let us concede that the sick dog pushes us to think of linked but opposed elements or sources of moving on: of moving on, not development. The opposed element to development causes the development to be dialectic, where I am using this word *dialectic* here in a narrow sense apparently different from what we talked about in, say, chapters 8, 9, and 10. The vet handles dialectic development in the dog in a manner that hopefully eliminates its effect on further dog development. But of course it remains part of the dog's story, part of the dog's system, and part of the dog. The dog, you surely concede, is not just the instant dog eyeing you delightedly today.

So we think vaguely—could you write down even one systematic proof of Euclid now, much less tell about Bertalanffy's school on the topic of systems, or even the smaller domain of mathematical logic that deals with systems and their incompletenesses?—of these few systems. But we are only touching the fringe of this *topos*, this place or way of being. These few system-types, after all, are embedded in myriads of ecosystems, themselves wound into an evolutionary flow. Have we defeated your imagination at this stage, or are you battling to hold it all together? Recall again our ramblings about **assemblies** in chapters 8, 9, and 10. The assembled dialecticians talked of in chapter 10 have to grapple together in psycho-chemical talk-tensions, towards advancing their communal clutch of improved imaging, their critical and creative effort clasped in the paws of mapping. Does their full effort not require some mapping-grip on evolution, lifting into some control the spread of Stephen Jay Gould's last great 1339-page effort, *The Structure of Evolutionary Theory*? Such a larger system weaves in a surrounding shadow of statistical systematics in its delicate limited effort to control randomness. We are in the world of F.M. Fisher, seeking "a rather grandiose picture of history," and leaning on a multiple Markov matrix imaging whose elements express, among other features, probability systematics relating $time_a$ and $time_b$.

And thus, if you have not given up reading, you perhaps find yourself bewildered at the searchings of these global professionals whose whats reach out over the net of history to meet its volleys. But at least you can think now imaginatively—recall histomaps, a fashion of the last century—to have a world map flowing through time, relatively stable now in land and sea, despite tides, tsunamis, earthquakes, and global warming-rhythms. Add now—I'm afraid that here we need to muse in terms of such innerpoint mappings as fibre bundle structures—a statistics of dispersings and the humility of fractal geometry, and we get slightly closer to the possibility of envisaging imaginatively the wriggling tubes of meanings and worldviews that overlap, converge, etc., in human history. Add, convenient to your needs, other explicitations such as the layers and flows of mice and men, minerals and moneys, musics and melancholies, and you begin to sense the cyclic reach of the A-Team.

I have mentioned a statistics of dispersal to which is connected at each world-point a statistics of possibilities. But that statistics is embedded in a realism of connecting t_x and t_{x+1}. There is, in A-Team heuristics imaging, the penumbra of possibilities surrounding the actual relativistically-related forward flows. This is entirely different from the idiocy of stringing people along in a farcical fantasy-land of parallel universes. Advanced quantum physics is tricky enough, and muddled enough about its concrete referencings, without floundering around in that farce.

I have been pushing along here, in doctrinal yet popular fashion, in an intimation of a geohistorical imaging that is to reach untold sophistications in future millennia—helped by nano- and biomimetic technologies and ranges of virtual representation. I have pushed along, indeed, in various writings to envisage this community arriving at an adequate population that has reached normal-law effectiveness, in a global population of ten billion, by the beginning of the tenth millennium. The push is part of the fantasy of "Arriving in Cosmopolis" (available in English and Spanish at: http://www.philipmcshane.ca/archives.html).

Now I ask you to pause with the question, Is this guy crazy? If you do in fact pause with it, then it is an is-question poised over a what-answer, an answer, descriptive or explanatory, reached by your whatting. I am suggesting here a what answer to what has to go on in history, and the what-answer is the zone of the group in the eight-cycle that focuses on the genetic what-need in history. That group can be understood by its simple paralleling with the experts round the sick pup. That group of vets have the back-up of a loose cycle of other competencies, and our group has the larger advantage of the collaborative cycle that rolls on to envisage effectively just how the swing pieces of the systems of history rescued by FS_7 are to be meshed by FS_8 to meet local needs and aspirations. I speak of rescuing and would note how creative that rescuing has to be: the dialectic elements have to be reversed in the full system so that the FS_7 system is a genetics of possibilities to be drawn on creatively by the final grouping. To that we turn in chapter 14.

Here we are concluding by gathering round, back to the wall of horrors at the beginning of this millennium, turning round, each of us, the question, is this guy crazy? The full craziness, yet in a sense the only craziness to be firmly mused on here, is the full system. I have skimmed along through varieties and meshings and layers of system, but the system that is at issue in this book and in our time is the full system that is the systematic cycling work of eight groups. On that I have skimmed along, with more color than adequacy, right through the book. The details of the sub-systems and of my optimism may seem crazy. The distant adequate populations in the cycling groups, running into millions, may certainly seem off the wall. But the question for you is: Is this guy crazy to pin our hopes on collaborating cyclically in this fashion?

So, I ask all along, but am asking you to home in on that asking here, for your view of the plausibility of this turn-around in the face of the needs of our back to the wall in the beginning of this millennium. I remind you of earlier chapters of the book by asking, what is your view? but dropping immediately the question mark. What is your view. In its full depth it is a what-to-be view: the what-is question is just a present flicker of that larger you and view. What is to be?: that is the issue that is to haunt this group of global reachers, omni-disciplinary but yet an integral neurochemistry of the reach forward to a scarcely-known edge that is a fresh take-off for shared whatting.

Forward to what, then? To more whatting of course, but a structuring whatting of global care. There is no pre-had genetics of this pup called human history. It is a self-creating fledgling with only a notion of flight in its micromuscled desire. The sparkle in this human bird of being is the eye-sparkle of its billions of chemo-whats. I wish you to pause as we head into musing on the final group, FS_8, and puzzle about the sparkle in your eye, your I: whether it is the sparkle of ontic adult growth and phyletic sunflowering, or an ineffective rebelliousness against, or the fightless settledness in, a globe of pseudo-democracies and arrogant tyrannies.

CHAPTER 14
STRUCTURING SYSTEMS IN TOWNS, GOWNS, AND CLOWNS

There is a deep sense in which this final eighth group of collaborators lives in the most refined tension of living. The sense, the deep reach, is best conveyed by the simple symbolism of thinking of the climb through any cycle—say in a generation—as a spiral. Or, more elementary still, image the eight groups as a 45° slope, a ladder starting from the ground of the present. No harm in adding here a useful image from a past effort: it is available on page 109 of *A Brief History of Tongue: From Big Ban to Coloured Wholes* (Halifax, Nova Scotia: Axial Press, 1998). The diagram is reproduced in its puzzling fullness on the next page, and the notes are left as they appear in the original text. It is an image that is worth bearing in mind in dealing with the complexifications that are to occur in the maturing of the cyclic system.

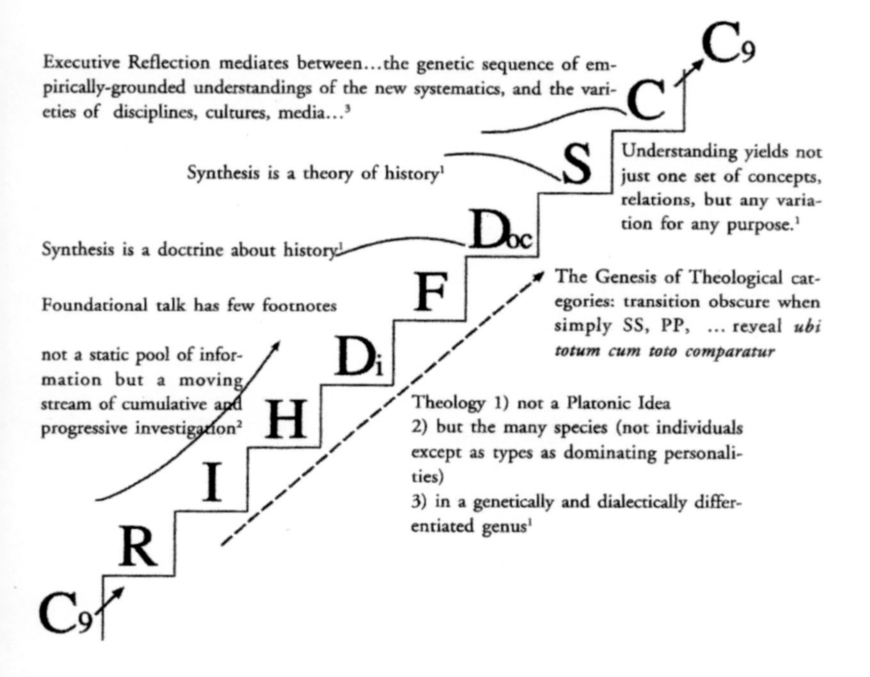

1. Bernard Lonergan, from unpublished notes of the early sixties available in the Toronto Lonergan center, Batch B, 8, 6, V.
2. Bernard Lonergan, "Christology Today: Methodological Reflections," *A Third Collection,* ed. Frederick E. Crowe, S.J. (Mahwah, NJ, Paulist Press, 1985), 82.
3. Philip McShane, "Systematics, Communications, Actual Contexts," *Lonergan Workshop*, vol. 6, ed. Frederick Lawrence (Chico, CA: Scholars Press, 1986), 151.

The diagram represents well the climb of the Tower people to new street meaning. The final eighth group has the challenge of somehow "dropping fresh meaning" to the ground floor so that the whole building rises in meaning, lifting Kansas towards a better glimpse of wonderland. We step back over two millennia for some further help to the beginning of the *Magna Moralia*, attributed to Aristotle. I quote the first paragraph.

> Since our purpose is to speak about matters to do with character, we must first inquire of what character is a branch. To speak concisely, then, it would seem to be a branch of nothing else than statecraft. For it is not possible to act at all in affairs of state unless one is of a certain kind, to wit, good. Now to be good is to possess the excellences. If therefore one is to act successfully in affairs of state, one must be of good character. The treatment of character then is, as it seems, a branch and starting-point of statecraft. And as a whole it seems to me that the subject ought rightly to be called, not Ethics, but Politics.

We ended the previous chapter with questions of politics, "of a globe of pseudo-democracies and arrogant tyrannies." It is that concrete global reality, or the cyclic improvements of it in future millennia, which is to be cherished in the contemplative struggles of this group. "How do we make the richer meaning of our entire cycling care somehow available to those who guide our days?" The group's task, then, is not a direct address of parents and politicians. It seeks to mediate the direct address of Town and Gown and Clown (the arts, the wits) by those who glocally contemplate and address these varieties of common living.

How can I possibly communicate briefly the complex richness of this solution to the problem of history's tadpole swimming? I could say that it is a matter of a two-step redemption of *haute vulgarization*, the redemption of the sort of stuff that is associated with the long-lived Fontenelle (1657-1757), the sort of stuff that is symbolized in our times by *Scientific American*. How is Group 8—a new G8!—to speak to the editors and writers of *Scientific American* so as to redeem the communications there from pretentious mythologizing? In its fullness the redemption calls for a patient genetic-dialectic climb to global **HOW**-languages, a newspeak that tells our nerves and bones who we are, what we are—recall the title to chapter 3—**H**omes **O**f **W**onder. I recall chapter 3, but I point to chapter 17, where we try another little seeding reach.

But as to brief communication, I must try some larger way that will not let us lose the momentum gathered in these last two chapters on a central doctrine of economics and on the massive reach to understand concrete systems that would mediate its control of bankers and tankers. Are we at sea here? Yes, and that is the clue that may carry us forward to the ocean of meaning of this specialty, an ocean of survival, a notion of survival. That last phrase brings to mind the chapter of that title, "The Notion of Survival," a chapter which concludes my little book of exactly forty years ago. It is available on my website so it helps my brevity here, and its full title is worth presenting here: *Wealth of Self and Wealth of Nations: Self-Axis of the Great Ascent*. And as I venture on with my analogy I would remind you that you are a notion of survival, an ocean of survival, and if you do not seek to be in this weird ballpark of Tower work, still you can get a sense of the game, enjoy the limber leaps, encourage excellence and, yes, lift your own local game. So let us all pause in our own way over the wonders of global water.

My own first serious pause over water was in the mid-1950s, when we flirted in our course work with Archimedes' *On Floating Bodies* but then got down to the serious stuff of a great work, *Hydrodynamics* written by Horace Lamb and published in 1897 in Cambridge. Close to 800 pages. The copy I worked with in 1953-54 was the sixth edition: obviously, therefore, a classic work of permanent value, like Archimedes' little book. Now let me leap a century from Lamb's book to 1997 and the four very substantial volumes that I have here on my desk, *The Collected Papers of Sir James Lighthill* from Oxford University Press (edited by M. Yousuff Hussaini). They contain his life's work on hydrodynamics.

But before I go on further about Lamb and Lighthill, let me show you where I am going in relation to economics and its politics and the sort of characters that are to emerge in this eighth group of cyclically collaborating collaborators. Already, through chapters 7 and 12, we may have got a slim doctrinal glimpse of the fundamental two flows of money and the back-up side-flows that connect with varieties of credit and the secondhand trade associated with the stock markets. Next we face the problem of global imaging of the two fundamental flows attached to which, obviously—but in strange topology—are the source and sink flows. Best just repeat myself here, from a previous reflection, Chapter 3 of *Sane Economics and Fusionism,* entitled "Imaging International Credit." As I promised, I omit footnotes within the text: we are reaching for a glimpse of an imaging of the global problem. IOC in the text refers to Randall D. Germain, *The International Organization of Credit: States and Global Finances in the World Economy*, Cambridge University Press, 1997.

"Now I must add the key image that I would suggest as dominating the immediate effort to glimpse the real problem of twenty-first century credit. It is an image that fits beautifully with the drive of **IOC** through history, but first envisages it ahistorically. The image in question, in our questing eye and kinesthetic sensibility, is an image of two spheres of micro-oscillations covering the globe. In its most elementary form it is a two-dimensional drawing of three closed circles, the two outermost being slightly irregular. Think of the inner circle as the surface of the earth, taken as uniform and watery. Then the next circle can be imagined as the ups and downs of the oceans' flows. But why the second such layered-in image of ocean flows?

Because we are imaging the actualities of any economy that we know of: two layers of flow, production goods and consumer goods. And that imaging, in its simplicity, is to be placed in the context of the global village's challenge to meet the promise of money: a concomitance of two flows, within the dynamics of our feeble human creativities that would gently lift our standard of pilgrim living to new unimaginable levels of love and leisure."

In conclusion, I return briefly to the challenge of luck and crisis talked of at the end of chapter 12. First there has to be the luck of some serious economists taking the elementary systematic base of the new doctrine seriously. This is a bit like our beginning chapter 1 with the dysfunctional family except that here the invitation is to view seriously a functional effort of innovative economics on a small island. I placed the beginning of that invitation in the end section of chapter 7. There one can arrive at the obvious destructiveness of the mismanagement of the financial flows. From that one can progress, but not without a great deal of historical and empirical work—a scrappy climb through the first four specialties—to a critique of present financial structures, known indeed to be rotten without there being a knowledge of **Why**? Again, we need the luck here of scrappy scrapping with Lobbies and Walls. But that luck is to be lifted by a sloping down from foundational wisdom, e.g., about villages and nations in the future, through doctrinal refinements and the consequent systematical enlargement that give ranges of possible moves from which ranges FS_8 seeks matches with local needs and capacities. And I note that that sentence is, yes, a dense metadoctrinal hint at an abundance of later work, a hint screaming for diagrams of sloping possibilities.

And to get a further sense of the long-term task of an economic science that is to deal, not with a single macro-innovation but with the Fourier complex of local microwaves and mesowaves, it is as well to return to my talk of the history of hydrodynamics and throw out some dates.

I talked of the gap of a century between that definitive work of Lamb (1897) and the lifework of Lighthill represented by the four volumes of 1997. As it happens, I was honored to edit the definitive work on economics in that year of 1997. It appeared in 1998 as volume 21 of *The Collected Works of Bernard Lonergan* with the title *For a New Political Economy*. What I wish you to fantasize about now is the emergence in economics of people like Lighthill during this next century so that there would be a population of such people— many of them in FS_8—generating equivalent types of dense essay, in 2097, on local empirical aspects of production and consumption. Then the macro-, meso- and micro- oscillations of economic innovations would be under the modest control of intelligence, in a beginning of a new promising history of money as promise.

CHAPTER 15
ELEMENTS OF FUTUROLOGY

You have now, I hope, a decent vague glimpse of the method of futurology as a cyclic collaboration of groups of people deeply, goal-keepingly, interested in effectively restructuring humanity's stumbling start. Yes, it is a fantasy, and if it is to be effective here and now it must add to that decent glimpse a fantasy of its own effective stumbling start. So we muse now over its growing, its **genetics** in an old use of that word. Imagine, perhaps, that we are dealing with something like a sunflower seed that we plant in unfavorable soil. But don't forget that, unlike the sunflower seed's planters, we have little idea of what is to emerge that is to be compared to the lofty eye-smile of the sunflower.

Let us take our fantasy in steps through these next four chapters. The fourth chapter, chapter 18, brings us to a modest pause over the possibility of futurology introduced in the Preface. We climb there by now thinking of getting the seed to be a shoot; next, in Chapter 16, courageously thinking of that getting as a robust science; and in chapter 17 we muse a little over some grim all-weather bothers and beasts that seek to make the sunflower's life unlivable.

Here we think positively about the seed's adaptive energy. Plant the sunflower seed 'upside-down' and it still reaches for the sun! Perhaps, indeed, we should now think of us as planting many seeds, in a reach for a sunflower forest. Yes, I mix messily metaphors, but come along for the Wonderland ride.

You ride all the better if you have had the experience of planting sunflowers, as my wife Sally and I have had in a previous Canadian Maritime life on the other, East, coast, doing daily walkabouts to see the uprising. So, the mixing of images leaves us with the task of seeding here and there the uprising that futurologists like us aim to foment, and doing walkabout within and without. Each of us has to plant where we are, in whatever upside-down way we can, starting inner walkabouts.

Notice that we are now in the zone of follow-through from the eighth specialty, FS_8, the zone that I regularly call C_9. This little book belongs in that zone, so there's a start of identification: especially as there is the ambiguity of this effort as being somehow foundational pedagogy, yet also doctrinal! The zone is that of commonsense exchange, and obviously another start is to make futurology a topic in that exchange, while media and mates and military may well be flooding us with misery. The seed is surrounded, not by ordinary manure—which obviously would help—but by the toxic effuse of bureaucracy and of the stalled conveniences of life and work.

In our illustrating of the cyclic process in the previous chapters our focus was on economic goings-on, and we paused over the murderous flow in various ways. Chapters 8, 9, and 10 made it a matter of personal escape and escapades with other like-minders. Here we consider the quieter cultivation of seeds of uprising. We each take whatting time to weigh up, even if only in commonsense fashion, the flow of what I chose to call mole-asses—and they are often malicious—as the flow hits our house or our heart. I invited you to home in there, on homelessnesses or homewreckings. No doubt you were too excited to pause in chapter 6 over the simple exercise of puzzling about not being at home with the A B C puzzle, caught as you were in the dance of this great idea, but now—or when you finished this can't-leave-it-down book—you need to face the personal challenge of getting beyond a cheery glimpse of dizzy heights to what is regularly a slow sweaty genetic—but messy—climb to a personal stand. If you are not up to facing that, well, at least pass along the book with a cheery face! But let us assume that you are up to more, that you are tired of mental oppression, mole-asses messing the byways of your **what**. Then the start of seeding comes uncomfortably home.

Isn't it all too easy to talk of a start that does not involve **my** starting?! We need to generate a community that is, so to speak, in on the start, ingesting the start so that we spontaneously talk startingly and startlingly. Might you, then, see and seize and be seized by the start of those three chapters, 8, 9, and 10, and the more precise start of chapter 11, so that you are the gentle but firm articulator, agricolator, of the seeds of a critical and constructive perspective? With chapter 10 there goes the challenge of not being alone in this, and of learning a new type of what-talk and how-talk which can be discomfortingly honest. But there was enough about that for starters in the two chapters 9 and 10. Note, though, that we are interested in the genetics of futurology and, on the side as it were, interested in understanding that genetics. Here we are right into that interest, that **whatting**, in that you now—or, as I must keep mentioning, when you finish your first enthusiastic read!—may take a fresh turn-around those chapters and find that indeed they are read better. This is a type of wedding, and as the first-ever Zulu book translated wisely claims, "The *isisusa* wedding dance is always appreciated by being repeated." Magema M. Fuze, "Prologue" to *Abantu Abamnyama: Lapa Bavela Ngakona* (*The Black People and Whence They Came: A Zulu View*), written around 1900, translated by Harry C. Lugg, University of Natal Press, 1979. So, you will have an instance of genetic growth to muse over in a dance round the dance that is fresh, Proustian, a creative remembrance. Or will you? The choice to leap out of present conventions is yours.

This realistic rambling musing helps to see the objective challenge better, and so let us carry on turning round the book in the book of ourselves. The chapters between 11 and 14 worded that objective challenge more particularly in the sick scenarios of contemporary economic exchanges, and the strategic start I envisage is in that domain. Even if external change is slow and grim and bloody, the internal change can step ahead of it in you and your strategic grouping. What can we do? We can do something about our own **what** in that zone so that, even if we throw bricks at Wall Streets, we do so informedly. At all events, I ask that some percentage of you—including you perhaps?—follow the exercises of chapters 9 and 10 with a serious effort to ingest the character of the group-projects of chapters 11-14. That serious ingesting, especially if shared, spontaneously gives rise to shifts in common meaning. Your shoot-growth may find its way to the printed page, the television camera, or the rangy realms of social media.

None of this seems to be the functional collaboration that has been our topic. But it can thus move to an emergence as common talk, seeding a backfiring to the need for FS_8. And it can cycle forward to freshen FS_1: "Is not a new start of economic science obvious in the distinction of two types of firm?" Students walked out of a class of a leading economist in Harvard last year, but they really did not know why. Branson gathers his Team B but really is at a loss for a coherent effective answer. So: you, now growing to know why, and the effective cyclic dynamic that would sustain that growth communally, can rise to walk and protest with a difference. And can begin to talk in creative protest. To whom you talk thus, creatively, persuasively: over to you, key elements in the creative surge, "Elements of Futurology."

The key elements in futurology's seed-shoot stage are slightly informed groups of global carers who effectively wish to get beyond Branson's Team B's perspective. Perhaps, indeed, there might be a weave into an alliance with that group or other such groups. It is to be a "futurologists without borders" grouping and yes, it needs doctors without borders and teachers without borders etc. But the core need is the need of a bent towards a fresh normative interpretation both of the flow of ones' own life and the flow of the economy. That tunes us to a sad snag in reaching for allies when you search concretely. For instance, I just cannot see Richard Branson and Arianne Huffington getting down to either discovering how economies really flow, locally or globally, and, wow, can you imagine them getting down seriously to appreciate their own **what**? I can state to them publically, as I do here and now, **What** is Richard; **What** is Arianna, but it would really blow my mind if I got an e-mail back from either looking for direction. Still, in this I could be Lucky, get lucky, without being Luciano: here's my e-mail, Tom, Dick and Arianna: pmcshane@shaw.ca. And I would note that I am quite content if they leave their **whats** as they are for the present, if only they and their associates would pause over the puzzle of the missing understanding at the heart of all political, financial, and business doings. Yes, we can agree, you, I, and they, that of course there is malice and corporate self-centeredness and greed. But surely seedling futurologists could get sufficiently competent to plant the creative destruction of the appalling ignorance in Economics 101?

Sometimes I think—as I did when I founded **SGEME**, "The Society for the Globalization of Effective Methods of Evolving"—that a focus on that issue, leaving aside serious self-understanding, would be a strategic way to go. And, indeed, I still think thus. We could focus-in like a sort of unified Wall Street movement or a Michael Moore following, but with a decent grip on the answer.

That was a basic reason why it seemed best to focus, in chapter 12, on doctrines that would counter the present dominant doctrine of profit in economics, and to that topic I shall return in chapter 18 and in the Epilogue. Here it seems better to wind to a conclusion thinking more broadly of the elements of seeding and shooting, since many of you readers are in other zones distant from the ballpark of changing economic education or behavior.

At the beginning of this chapter I very deliberately used the word *genetics* when it would have been easier to use the word *development*. Talk of development in a great deal of botany and zoology is in terms of genetic codes and chemical information, not about the strange shifting of patterns that leads to quite new forms: the frog swims quite differently from the tadpole. Discussions of human development, of you and me growing, are not really much better. Psychologists tend to be invited to focus on those among us that are evidently psychically-crippled. But there have been odd people like Abraham Maslow and Candace Pert who puzzle over the dynamics of our better growing. Still, there is no loud call for, or of, a shift up from Maslow's gloomy statistic, "less than 1% of adults grow." What, then, of adults growing together? What might seed that growth? Here I have skimmed along in a way that satisfies neither you nor me. It is a Zulu question, answered, in the days of the book I mentioned above, by elderhood. The tribe dance freshly a second time; the younger members can sit round a fading fire listening to and through grandmother's tales of the tribe as if they were quite startlingly new; Proust twists and turns to alert us to the freshness of a tune or of the taste of tea. But these are not worlds we live in. I write, then, of growing and understanding growing, but we have no molecular grip on that reality, its problems or its hopes.

What might seed hope. Full stop! Yes! But **what** is controlled by the madnesses of our dead cultures that kill off human growth in the name of a myth of economic growth and its silly servant full employment. What then, **what** then, of adult growth, Oriental or Zulu or Proustian? Imagine that it could be an accelerating thing, that you could become wondrously a stranger to yourself of last month, that you and your mate could rise to being ever-freshly strangers, beginners in whatting. There, now, is an imagining! It is quite out of kilter with the ethos of our modern times, which subtly seek a stale steadiness of humanity, something to be tinkered into a global stability that is as evident as roads and annually-fresh automobiles and large international trading trucks and tricks and tanks a million.

The futurology express is to seed quite different shoots rising to a sunflower smile, a radiance of a global community that is laced with a realism about its feebleness and its faults. Will swords disappear in favor of ploughshares as *Isaiah* 2:4 has it? Well, at least we will have left the crippled bustling tadpole of the beginning of this millennium far behind in an—at present—undreamable leisure; our children's grandchildren will COPON with a radical newness; and our adult descendants will be elders and not, as Proust found (the conclusion of *Remembrance of Things Past*), "not old folk but young people of eighteen, very much faded."

CHAPTER 16
FUTUROLOGY AS SCIENCE

We carry forward here, in brief descriptive summary, the task of chapter 9, the articulation of who and what I am if I am a worker in the Tower. Yet, as I begin this chapter I sense that this is a bit like asking Molly Bloom to tell, What do you do when you say "Yes, Yes, Yes" at the end of Joyce's *Ulysses*? or asking Amy Winehouse to plainly state, What do you mean when you sing "No, No, No" in the middle of *Rehab*? So should I sing, swing, or slice and dice with my hand in my blooming winehouse, taking a stand in this rehab land, when I darkly express Futurology's Express: "Futurology is the conception, affirmation, and effecting of the integral heuristic structure of history"?[5]

Futurology is: caring as best I can, as best we can, for the pup, the shoot, called history. So, in it, we need to struggle to be cyclically up-to-date, in this early stage of human history—as best we can—regarding the carers and abusers in our story, regarding their care and abuse of our Galactic flight. All we have is our rambling minding of that story of care and abuse so far, the story of a dysfunctional family in the pre-adolescence of a tadpole with no suspicion of the frog to come. Yet, yes, yes, yes, "heart going like mad and yes I said yes I will yes,"[6] there is history to be made.

And that making pivots on the **what** in the heart being aloud and loud in going like mad, round and round, expressing futurology's express.

"What anthem did Bloom chant partially in anticipation of that multiple, ethnically irreducible consummation?

[5] A modification of the definition of metaphysics of *Insight: A Study of Human Understanding, Collected Works of Bernard Lonergan*, vol. 3, ed. Frederick Crowe and Robert Doran (Toronto: University of Toronto Press, 1992), 416 (hereafter, *Insight*). I will abbreviate the *Collected Works of Bernard Lonergan* below as *CWL*.
[6] The conclusion of Molly Bloom's speech at the end of James Joyce's *Ulysses*.

Kolod balejwaw pnimah
Nefesch, jehudi, homijah.

Why was the chant arrested at the conclusion of this first distich? In consequence of defective mnemotechnic.

How did the chanter compensate for this deficiency? By a periphrastic version of the general text."

I could well invite you to travel back with me round and round this quotation from the second last section of *Ulysses,* with its expansive whatting.[7] "With what meditations did Bloom accompany his demonstration to his companion of various constellations? / Meditations of evolution increasingly vaster: of the moon invisible in incipient lunation, approaching perigree: of the infinite lattiginous scintillating uncondensed milky way..."

Might it not awaken your *what*?

For it is not true that we have no suspicion of the frog to come.

What is our glorious creative suspicion. Full stop. End of highest diving board. Poise on your paws, loop the lunatic loop, and create the next higher diving board.

"My daddy thinks I'm fine" (Amy Winehouse, *Rehab*). Your daddy, present culture's idiot leadership, your daddy thinks you're fine. More automobiles and pills, work and leisure daze, more G_8s, G_{20}s etc., more unfree trade, and more $$$ at the top, just bank on it! "And you get to vote for us now and then." But something stirs you beyond protest to rescue your hearty whatting. That stirring is the Big Bang in your molecular what.

The stirring is to be our Yes and No, fermenting into an underwhirl, like the cultural Vorticism of a hundred years ago, dreamed up by Ezra Pound and Wyndam Lewis, but now

---

[7] The section of *Ulysses* from which I quote is a series of questions and answers.

effective; like *La Spirale,* the last dream-book of Flaubert, but hitting the press core. Might we think of it as that wonder of the world, the Bellrock Lighthouse, east of Scotland, rising out of the waters, poised on a rock, two hundred years ago? The brazen waters of our times tide around our shabby scaffolding as we begin to raise up our Tower, hoping for circulating light, "a ruddy gem of changeful light" that will still be seen in later times.

I write thus, with the romanticism of Robert Stevenson—not *that* R.L.S.!—who dreamed that Lighthouse Tower and battled his way beyond bureaucracy, a small rodent of 1800 that sits now mature and complacent, a Godzilla of G numbers and G-men.

Some few, maybe you, have to withdraw from saying, singing, dancing, thus saying No, in their own way, a way that yet can ferment to an ever-richer what.[8] But there is needed a mad group of Yes-sayers that ferment their whats in what I might call a **W** world. We need W-numbers[9] but might you also notice the twist

---

[8] The slow cultural intussusception and incarnation of the answers to "what's what?" and "what's the economy?" may bubble forward in this century. The book *The Future as Cultural Fact* (see note 1 of the Preface), which fails to raise either question, nonetheless opens up psychic contexts for the emergence of the questions and their answers.

[9] The question of symbolism, always aesthetic in its quest and in its objectification, is a huge topic that I decided, near the end of this work, to avoid. I have included my W-words, $\mathbf{W_i}$ as I call them, but minimally. The "more on symbols" promised at the end of chapter 6 is thus reduced to this note. For an incomplete list of $\mathbf{W_i}$, see *Prehumus* 2 (available at http://www.philipmcshane.ca/prehumous-02.pdf). The central symbol of this little book is in fact $\mathbf{W_3}$, a simplified version of which is what I call *The Tower of Able,* constructed from W_3 by doing a cut-out and building a three dimensional image. That image, titled *Lonergan's Dream,* is given on page 163 of Pierrot Lambert and Philip McShane, *Bernard Lonergan: His Life and Leading Ideas* (Vancouver: Axial Publishing, 2010). One can compare it to the Lighthouse Image that is the Frontispiece. But, better, one can construct one's own image of the Tower, make it taller like the lighthouse, perhaps adding a spiral staircase all the way up on the outside instead of the short visible stair of the real lighthouse. The achievement of futurology is to be a sufficient population of lighthouses and keepers and builders radiating light cyclically and spirally.

of a terrible pun? We need the freshness of liberated W_0–men.[10] Yes indeed Molly, you have a point in that speech that rambles round the Rock of Gibraltar: "I don't care what anybody says it'd be much better for the world to be governed by the women in it you wouldn't see women going and killing one another."

I take a pause here and discern this deviation from my intended swing into the description of the foundations of the science of futurology and I realize that the deviation indeed has its place, and it leads me now to turn us round, back to the wall, in a different way and sway for the rest of the book.

We are in chapter 16 of this little book, but not really. Really we are hovering over or vortexting, spiraling, round chapter 16 of a much bigger book. There are those of my readers who knew that already, indeed some who could sniff the odd twirling of the table of contents. The bigger book is *Insight*, and the title of its sixteenth chapter is "Metaphysics as Science." That chapter was written sixty years ago by the old guy I talked about earlier[11] as having indicated to me the structure of futurology thirteen years later—1966—than the writing of his chapter 16. What, then, am I doing here, or was doing till I diverted at the beginning of this chapter? I was trying to weave his later expression of his discovery of futurology into his previous big book.[12] And those in the know may already have noticed the cunning of the weave: I'll get back to that in the Epilogue. But there is a freedom now for me in that the chat is out of the bag. I'll maintain the chat in its brief descriptive form, but now you can nurse the possibility of definitely following up this futurology in a fuller fashion if you feel the urge. Recalling Robert Stevenson, I need sixty good folk—

[10] Yes, a terrible twisted pun, but there is a dynamic in feminism that can rescue culture if it is not devoured by the tentacles of various warps cultivated by deviant patriarchies.
[11] In chapter 1, on page 11.
[12] The weaving is a topic of the Epilogue.

more women than men—to set sail towards the East for the start of a building on that Bell Rock.

With the chat out of the bag I can note a strategy that I have used over the years when pointing towards Lonergan's searchings and achievements: I pick a particular writing or chapter of his and give some probing comments regarding a part of a paragraph or even a phrase. So, here, the obvious zone of chapter 16 of *Insight* is the final section 5, a little over eight pages, "Metaphysics as Science." And here, too, is the heart of my reach, my thesis, my pointing: it is simply expressed in the change of title to "Futurology as Science." But the meaning is far from simple: its meaning is of a spiraling of effective light that leaves behind all the old moods and modes associated with the word *metaphysics*. Yet the leaving behind is there, in Lonergan's text. "Such a procedure eliminates mere disputation and bestows upon metaphysics the status of a science."[13] But muse now: what did he mean by 'such a procedure' in that statement? All along he knew he had a problem, the problem that lurks in the word 'eliminates.'[14] On the turn of the page he makes the point, sitting under his Newtonian apple tree. "As in the natural sciences, so also in metaphysics, an understanding of the method, its accurate formulation, its acceptance, and its proper use, are neither automatically achieved nor automatically efficacious."[15] The apple, the moon, the penny, swing down and round into his neurochemistry thirteen years later, but then the need to chant faltered in his tired throat. "What anthem did Bloom chant partially in anticipation of that multiple, ethnically irreducible consummation? Why was the chant arrested at the conclusion of this first distich? In consequence of defective mnemotechnic. How did the chanter compensate for this deficiency? By a periphrastic version of the general text." The

---

[13] *Insight*, *CWL* 3, 549.

[14] It is the full problem of Cosmopolis raised mainly in the concluding section of chapter 7 of *Insight*.

[15] *Insight*, *CWL* 3, 550.

version, far from periphrastic, packed the text of *Insight* into the list that I mentioned in our bankrupt chapter 11, the list that runs from (1) to (9).[16] In his weariness he skipped past (10) and left (11) aside, a piece, at all events, of (6). But he knew his chant was plainsong in search of a symphony and so he points to the high-dive board in the next paragraph: "from such a broadened base one can go on"[17] to give a symphonic version of the light plaintive humming of the first four chapters of his book. The task remains, the rock[18] identified on which to Tower the light: he had successfully battled "to secure a firm orientation and a tendency that in the long run is efficacious."[19] He invited others mercilessly to the rock firmness: "To say it all with the greatest brevity, it is not only to read *Insight* but to discover oneself in oneself."[20]

My effort in this little book is the much more modest one of nudging you to find that battered *what* that is you, battered by "the monster that has stood forth in our day."[21] It is an almost impossible task in our present cultures, yet your feeble rescue-efforts, if you will to make them, are to found the Light Tower of Futurology, even if you only stand informedly, slightly aside from the madding crowd, shouting encouragement for what, after all, is to give COPON hope for your children's children.

---

[16] The list of *Method in Theology* (Toronto: University of Toronto Press, 2003), 286-7 challenges the reader to climb through the self-discovery pointed to in the book *Insight*. My replacement of *Insight's* early chapters by the drive for futurology is an additional challenge that weaves into and around the previous challenge. For the fuller contemporary Christian challenge, relating to the special categories of *Method* page 291, see note 95 in the Epilogue.

[17] *Method in Theology*, 187.

[18] "There is then a rock on which one can build." *Method in Theology*, 19; and in the note there he remarks, "It will become evident in Chapter Four that the more important part of the rock has not yet been uncovered." Lonergan is talking here of the rock that is the deep conviction of "a friendly universe." *Ibid.*, 117, line 13. That rock I write of in chapter 20, but my weave round the metaphor of rock in this book is more complex than his.

[19] *Insight*, *CWL* 3, 549-50.

[20] *Method in Theology*, 260.

[21] *Ibid.*, 40.

"Standing naked to the world 120 feet above the sea outside on the balcony is a novel experience to say the least."[22]

[22] Charlie Riding, *A Quiet Night in the Bell Rock Lighthouse*, 1998.

CHAPTER 17
FUTUROLOGY AS DIALECTIC

The dialectic problem of futurology, of the Tower of Able, of the Bell Tower on the battered rocks, is to effectively reveal and rescue the truth of history, against all odds and oddities. The oddities, in their mix of stupidity and cupidity, generate myths instead of factual accounts, thus lying about the course of events and grounding misinterpretations of humanity's hopes and meanings.

One would expect, then, a coherent reflection on the dialectic either of metaphysics or of futurology to tackle the tasks of [1] identifying myths, [2] identifying lies, and [3] identifying misinterpretations. So, one finds three sections in the seventeenth chapter of Lonergan's *Insight* pivoting on [1] mystery as opposed to myth, [2] truth as opposed to lies, and [3] interpretation as opposed to misinterpretation.

My switch of style in chapter 16 enables me to make this connection here, thus revealing the twining of my chapters with those of Lonergan's major works, *Insight* and *Method in Theology*. But it also enabled me to recall and implement a previous style of commenting on those works and to add notes. My commenting avoids summary and so generally homes in on a section or a page. Here I home in on a single paragraph of the parallel chapter, one conveniently named *60910*.[23] The focus and the footnoting allow me, in the present case, to handle all three problems identified above in a fashion that challenges superficial or merely doctrinal treatment.

The next chapter will take up the issue of "against all odds": are the odds too much for us? Here I wish to pause over two oddities. There is first the oddity about which there may seem perhaps a

[23] The paragraph spans pages 609 and 610 of *Insight*.

disproportionate amount of chat in this little book. But it is a massive oddity: the dominant ethos of military-industrial-educational alliances of all colors with a mindless cluster of economic oversights, alliances that keep some of us hungry, some of us pampered, and all of us busy and ignorant. More, certainly, should be said about that global monster, but here my attention turns to a seemingly different oddity: the oddity of a so-called following of Lonergan that is usually titled Lonerganism. On that, too, I have expressed my views, but not here, so far. At least, not explicitly. But there is a sense in which the group is there, with most of the rest of us, victims of the culture that is busily embedded in a flow of informedness that passes, in its abundance of reference and aesthetic weavings, for serious understanding. The challenge posed either by the list (1) – (9), or by that final section of chapter 16 of *Insight*, leaves them secretly baffled.[24] Chapter 17 is virgin territory for many.[25] Section 3 of 17 is, perhaps, to be regarded as far-out craziness.[26]

The core issue here, for futurology, is the effective genesis of presentational pedagogy that will break forward from the mythology of *haute vulgarization* to the unknowing that grounds

---

[24] I recall one of the leading Lonergan experts expressing such bafflement to me in a search for guidance. Good will is not enough in present theology: the shift demanded is a dreadful attack on the deeper molecular habits of old-style training. Recall my various rambles on the axial superego, e.g., *Humus* 2: "*Vis Cogitativa*: Contemporary Defective Patterns of Anticipation" (available at: http://www.philipmcshane.ca/humus-02.pdf).

[25] I think now sadly of the conference in Concordia University that gave rise to the volume *Lonergan's Hermeneutics: Its Development and Application*, edited by Sean E. McEvenue and Ben F. Meyer (Washington D.C.: The Catholic University of America Press, 1989). We just did not get near chapter 17 of *Insight*.

[26] "Here I am eccentric enough to compare Lonergan's effort with Donizetti's, indeed to compare *Insight* with Donizetti's *Lucia di Lammermoor*. There is the 'mad scene' near the end of the Opera which I like to compare with the madness of Lonergan's treatment of Interpretation near the end of his Opus. Lonergan's madness, the heart of his new view, remained unsung throughout the twentieth century." I quote from *FuSe Zero*, "A Simple Appeal for Functional Collaboration" (available at: http://www.philipmcshane.ca/fuse-00.pdf).

genuine whatting. *Haute vulgarization* is identified by Lonergan in a discomforting manner worth drawing attention to here. He prefaced his brief remarks, in an essay on "Exegesis and Dogma," with an indication of "fuller indications in *Insight*, chapter 17, on the truth of interpretation."[27] On the next page he attacks the subtle closure to theory that is in fact massively present in our culture: "the broader simplifications offered" display regularly that the talker was "never bitten by theory."[28] In another essay, "Time and Meaning," he has a lengthier criticism of theory's "devalued acknowledgement"[29] by this gross cultural ignorance, "lost in some no-man's land between the world of theory and the world of common sense."[30] The deep educational issue is that such a culture "gives an illusion of knowledge, a false idea of what science is. And it clutters the mind."[31]

There are many twists of pedagogical presentations relevant to breaking forward from such mythic common sense to a common sense tuned to the unknown of self and others, but I wish here only to point to the significance of symbolism when that symbolism is meshed psychically with a valued acknowledgement of its meaning. Let me begin by quoting Lonergan's prose expression of his hopes for metaphysics or, as I prefer, futurology. Think of him as writing about the genesis of the adequate Tower person. "So it comes about that the extroverted subject visualizing extension and experiencing duration gives place to the subject orientated to the objective of

[27] Lonergan, *Philosophical and Theological Papers, 1958-64* (Toronto: University of Toronto Press, 1996), *CWL* 6, 154.

[28] *Ibid.*, 155. I add his next comment which brings us back to our suggestion about imitating Newton in our struggle with economics. "[H]e has no apprehension, no understanding, for example, of the fact that Newton spent weeks in his room in which he barely bothered looking at his food, while he was working out the theory of universal gravitation." *Ibid.*

[29] *Philosophical and Theological Papers*, 1958-64, *CWL* 6, 121.

[30] *Ibid.*

[31] *Topics in Education* (Toronto: University of Toronto Press, 1993), *CWL* 10, 145. He is talking here, illustratively, of ignorance of the meaning of d^2s/dt^2.

the unrestricted desire to know and affirming beings differentiated by certain conjugate potencies, forms, and acts grounding certain laws and frequencies."[32] Do not be distressed about the full meaning here: just think of form as mentioned and muse over the simple question, "What form are you in?" *Haute vulgarization* might invite you to mention tiredness or exuberance or impatience: "sufficient for the day is the newspaper thereof," recalling a Joyce saying. But, really, what form are you in, in your "molecules of emotion," your amygdalic stress, whatever?[33] It is as well to take the 'whatever' out of the dark by symbolizing the form of forms that you are. How about you as $f(p_i ; c_j ; b_k ; z_l ; u_m ; r_n)$?[34]

That neat little formula, which I call W_1, offers a salvific base to talk of you, where "of" works both ways. It leans towards meeting two demands of Bernard Lonergan, both challenges to his disciples. There is the demand for adequate symbolization: "If we want to have a comprehensive grasp of everything in a unified whole, we shall have to construct a diagram in which are symbolically represented all the various elements on the question along with all the connections between them."[35] There is the demand for being up with the times: "… the defenders are left in the unenviable position of always arriving on the scene a little breathlessly and a little late."[36]

---

[32] *Insight, CWL* 3, 537.

[33] "Molecules of emotion" obviously brings to mind the work of Candace Pert. On the amygdala's role in reception and response: Google the literature.

[34] This is the first of a series of supportive images. See the text at the following note, fuller in the original regarding the need for supportive imaging. See also note 9 above.

[35] Lonergan, *The Ontological and Psychological Constitution of Christ* (Toronto: University of Toronto Press, 2002) *CWL* 7, 151. See note 9 above.

[36] *Insight, CWL* 3, 755. Add to this the clear brutal scientific demands made on pages 3-4 and 350-351 of *Method in Theology*.

We can return now to the "comeabout" quotation, thinking of the **comeabout** as the regular cycling[37] of the functional efforts, and see a concrete source of the genesis of an eightfold team tuning each other up to par.[38] The talkers and the talked about are lifted luminously into being unknowns, unknown beings on the way in history. They are the tadpole, moving towards being an unknown frog, nudged towards the suspicion that the future is not just a bigger tadpole by studies of the early tadpole genetics.

But "on the way in history" has two meanings.[39] Think back to the veterinary experts. They are on the way (2) in the story through their education, which continues: but they are also on the way (1) towards caring for the puppy. And surely a bit from the previous footnote is worth musing over: "(2) aims at expressing knowledge of history," and (1) aims at expressing history. Have we not two meanings of expressing to hold together?

---

[37] See the text at note 32 and place it in the following context supplied by Lonergan. "That circle—the systematic exigence, the critical exigence, and the methodical exigence—is also a genetic process. One lives first of all in the world of community and then learns a bit of science and then reflects, is driven towards interiority to understand precisely what one is doing in science and how it stands to one's operations in the world of community. And that genetic process does not occur once. It occurs over and over again. One gets a certain grasp of science and is led onto certain points in the world of interiority. One finds that one has not got hold of everything, gets hold of something more, and so on. It is a process of spiraling upwards to an ever fuller view." *Early Works on Theological Method* (Toronto: University of Toronto Press, 2010), *CWL* 22, 140.

[38] The vortex movement of the science is to have two effects: a spinning in of the competent and serious; a spinning out of the people not up to the strange in-climbing involved. The spin-out group thus, paradoxically, are invited to rise to larger personal achievements of expressing history, ontically and phyletically.

[39] "The word *history* is employed in two senses. There is history (1) that is written about and there is history (2) that is written. History (2) aims at expressing knowledge of history (1)." *Method in Theology*, 175. It is perhaps of interest to note that it is from pondering over this first sentence of Lonergan's first chapter on history in this book, against the background of my searching for a fuller meaning of "history in the style of Burckhardt rather than Ranke" (*ibid.*, 250) that the idea of a book on **expressing history** came to me.

So, if we wish to best express, hasten, the heath of a puppy or of history we need to aim at excellence in (2). What is that excellence? We have already talked of it in relation to the vets; indeed we wound that talk round the need in the carers of history. But let us bring that weaving into the context of the care talked about by Lonergan in the third part of his 17th chapter of *Insight*. So I come to my selected paragraph, 60910. I should quote it in full, even though, like the **comeabout** quotation, it contains some bothersome phrases.

"The explanatory differentiation of the protean notion of being involves three elements. First, there is the genetic sequence in which insights gradually are accumulated by man. Secondly, there are the dialectical alternatives in which accumulated insights are formulated, with positions inviting further development and counterpositions shifting their ground to avoid the reversal they demand. Thirdly, with the advance of culture and of effective education, there arises the possibility of the differentiation and specialization of modes of expression; and since this development conditions not only the exact communication of insights but also the discoverer's own grasp of his discovery, since such grasp and its exact communication intimately are connected with the advance of positions and the reversal of counterpositions, the three elements in the explanatory differentiation of the protean notion of being fuse into a single explanation."[40]

I quote this discomforting paragraph in full because it is, to my mind, the crisis paragraph of the book *Insight*.[41] It is a dense doctrinal statement, and books will emerge struggling with its meaning in particular disciplines and in the reach for comprehensive omnidisciplinary historical control. What might I helpfully say at the conclusion of this chapter?

---

[40] *Insight*, *CWL* 3, 609-10.

[41] My little book, *The Road to Religious Reality* (Vancouver: Axial Publishing, 2012) pivots on its meaning.

Tackle that paragraph by thinking of the notion of the pup, and the hunt for a single explanation of its ongoing health. There is the genetic sequence of views accumulated over time on the pup. Secondly, there are the other wrong views in history that still may be picked over to add to the genetic sequence. Thirdly, such talk about the pup's health has changed a great deal even in the past century. The assembled expert vets—and we have stumbled about with them in previous chapters—have managed to push towards a single view accepted in pup-science.

But you see, of course, that this past paragraph simply nudges you to set out towards illustrations of 60910. We are here only at the beginning of this business of fusing, not just the pup, but the history of pups and everything else, into a single explanation. And, not mentioned explicitly here, we must not forget that the pup itself, perhaps occasionally hungry and ill-treated, is a genetic and dialectic sequence of neurochemical patterns. So: we are back to the start that we mused over in chapter 15.

CHAPTER 18
THE POSSIBILITY OF FUTUROLOGY

The advantage of the switch of style and intent in chapter 16 enables us to move forward with a larger context in mind. That larger presence in mind will vary enormously, depending on your background. You may be an interested beginner; you may be a Lonergan scholar of serious standing. I wish here to cater for all types, and so the flow of the chapter is to be as independent as possible from the fuller context that I have in mind and that I struggle with as I push towards the end of the book, whose chapters run parallel to the same number chapters of *Insight*.[42] The Epilogue, too, is in parallel. Further, there is a parallel with *Cantowers* 18-21 on my website, with *Cantower* 21 expressing the parallel through its odd title, "Epilodge."[43]

Yet there is a strange weaving of problems together in this chapter that sets it apart. It is present there, as a challenge, in the two titles of this chapter and the 18th chapter of *Insight*: "The Possibility of Ethics" is replaced by "The Possibility of Futurology." But it is also present in the challenge that I have left myself from other chapters here. There is the most immediate such challenge coming from my 17th chapter's avoidance of the topic of Truth, which occupies the middle section of Lonergan's *Insight* 17. The topic of truth, however, is twined into the drive of *Insight*'s central chapters, 9–14, and is focused crisply in that dread-filled reader's choice of page 413, lines 6–12: "It will be a basic position (1) if the real is the concrete universe of being and not a subdivision of the 'already out there now'; (2) if the subject becomes known when it

---

[42] My effort to cater for all types is helped by my footnoting. For the beginner, things to follow up. For old hands perhaps just the recollection of familiar connections and problems, but also things to follow up.

[43] The three previous *Cantowers* also have odd titles: *Cantower* 18, "The Possibility of Cultural Ethics"; *Cantower* 19, "Ultimates"; *Cantower* 20, "Intimates." (The *Cantower* series is available at: http://www.philipmcshane.ca/cantowers.html). We shall muse over the suggested shifts of meaning as we move along.

affirms itself intelligently and reasonably and so is not known yet in any prior 'existential' state; and (3) if objectivity is conceived as a consequence of intelligent inquiry and critical reflection, and not as a property of vital anticipation, extroversion, and satisfaction."[44] In contrast, I have maintained a focus right through this little book on the subject as **what**, as whatting, as to-do-whatting.

I return to the problem caught in the two titles, "The Possibility of Futurology" and "The Possibility of Ethics," add my *Cantower* 18 title of ten years ago, "The Possibility of Cultural Ethics," and latch on some musings on Lonergan's discovery of 1965.

As I pondered over how to handle the latch-on, I returned to the 2003 reflections, in *Cantower* 18, of the younger me and found, find, that the conclusion, on page 2 to the Introduction to those reflections, hits the point adequately. The point was the twist, in *Cantower* 18's 3rd section, of the third section of *Insight* 18. The twist was to bring out the shift in ethical discovery processes, including the ethics of the processes of theology. I omit footnotes given there.

> The man Lonergan paused, for a decade after *Insight*, in his **capacity** and **need** to reach a hearty answer to the unlife that he and his contemporaries were leading in Rome, in the world: "the setting is magnificent; the lighting superb; the costumes gorgeous; but there is no play." *Insight*, *CWL* 3, 262. He conceived of an **institution**, with its **roles** and **tasks**, which could transform that pretentious evil misery, thus identifying a new ethics of cultural reflection on culture. The finality of that identity cries out in each of our molecules.

I shall display the context referred to there in boldface, the display of words on *Method in Theology* page 48, presently. But key to the

[44] *Insight*, *CWL* 3, 413.

ethical shift I am nudging us towards all along is the manner in which, among Lonergan's scribbles of that 1965 February, there is included a return to Thomas' beginning of the *Summa*. Lonergan was luminously leaping beyond axiomatics to a non-foundational cyclic theology. He had arrived, in that slow-burned leap, at "The Truth of Interpretation," where now interpretation is to take on a remote radiant meaning. How does one caringly interpret the tadpole's growing when there is little but a promise of its life-moves towards croaking? The promise is there clouded by tribal meanings. How are we to sift through those discerningly so as to leave the tale of the tadpole's swim and arrive at frogdom come?

My annoying puns have a point. We desperately need to flip and flex our feeble imaginations and our whattings if we are to envisage and bring forth effectively, as adults, The Democracy of Humans instead of mumbling to God, in a sort of childish helplessness, "Thy Kingdom Come."[45]

I strayed, in that previous paragraph, into my Epilogue, so let me return to the perspective that I inherited from Lonergan's *Insight*, the perspective of **what's** authentic climb. There are subtleties about this perspective that I leave to the Epilogue. What I wish to do here is secularize two zones of Lonergan's writing, one in *Insight* and one in *Method*. I do so with the beginners in mind.

---

[45] Obviously, I am not here rejecting prayer, but the childishness that is caught in the joke about the chap stranded in the flood praying for help while boats pass. Adult humanity can still sing Newman's "Lead Kindly Light" when it cherishes effectively the light that leads within, Jeremiah's law in the heart (*Jeremiah* 31:31-34). On the challenge to bring forth an adult spirituality see note 95 below. One seeks to move through history in the dynamic clasp of the Spirit expressing [that word again!], with and within the Incarnate Word, the story of the Kingdom. This theological perspective reaches way beyond N.T. Wright's effort in *How God Became King* (New York: Harper, 2012).

First, there is the meaning of "Is? Is! Is," in *Insight*.[46] When I think of the possibility of futurology I think of the move up the scale of probability for the positioning of *Insight* in the Tower community. The serious possibility of futurology pivots on that core and its fallout, or rather fall-in,[47] being a taken-for-granted in ongoing creative dialogue. It would be foolish of me to do some juggle-summary here about this. It is a core that requires a massive pedagogical effort; indeed it requires the Tower Whirl through these next centuries.

Secondly, there is the meaning of the word-Spread on page 48 of *Method*. It too will need the Tower Whirl, but now the Whirl spins into the Spread. But I should put the Spread in here for my beginner-readers:

Individual		*Social*	*Ends*
Potentiality	*Actuation*		
capacity, need	operation	cooperation	particular good
plasticity, perfectibility	development, skill	institution, role, task	good of order
liberty	orientation, conversion	personal relations	terminal value

---

[46] I recall conversations with Lonergan during Easter of 1961 and the summer of 1971 where I asked him about this, in particular, "when did you get clear on the meaning of is?" His reply, "when I got that far in *Insight*." The communal reaching of that FAR is a task of the whirl of functional collaboration in these next centuries.

[47] I follow up on the previous note. The vortex of collaboration is to spin-in a fall-in group that is in that strange world of luminous self-solitude pointed to in the brief description given at note 45 above. The fallout group generally can live in the world in which 'ordinary realism', not talked about, is a legitimate symbol. Common sense should not be expected to reach refined self-luminousness in these next few millennia. Contemporary students of Lonergan should not expect to position themselves properly by reading *Insight*. On this see *Cantower* 9, 'Position, Poisition, Protopossession" (available at: http://www.philipmcshane.ca/cantower9.pdf)

The Tower Whirl is to be in there, right in the center of the *Social*, a network of institutions, roles, tasks, a strange topological unit hovering over land and sea, calling and cauling each capacity, need, "a need to respond to a further reality than meets the eye and to grope [our] way towards it,"[48] but twirling longingly in and round a whatting regarding and guarding the Spread's last line content of personal relations in their liberties, reorientations, and ultimates.

Layers and levels of conversions are in that whirling future whirling, but three are twirled round you in this little book, themselves intertwined. These are the institutions of promise that are to be banked into the proper cycling of minding and of money and of meaning.

There is a sense, indeed, in which I am playing the role of Schumpeter's bankers here, who, if they are doing things right in these present times, "make themselves thoroughly unpopular with governments, politicians and the public,"[49] and indeed with academics—alas, most paradoxically, among academics, particularly with those who claim to be disciples of Lonergan.

The Tower is to spin round the ocean of common meaning, like the light of the Bell Lighthouse, those three lifts of minding, money, and meaning, so that futurology might cut continuously through the brutal myths of the ordinary and the commercial. At the center there is the deepening mystery of the meaning of what, what self-revealed not only in its ontic *oneness*—but also in its phyletic *claritas*. Then, indeed, we will have sniffed the ethical cigar![50]

---

[48] I quote from the center of the powerful end-paragraph of *Insight*, *CWL* 3, 639.
[49] Joseph Schumpeter, *Business Cycles: A Theoretical, Historical, and Statistical Analysis of the Capitalist Process* (New York: McGraw Hill, 1939), volume 1, 118.
[50] I am thinking here of James Joyce's exposition of Aquinas' view of beauty as involving integrity, harmony, and radiance. It is about fifty pages from the end of *A Portrait of the Artist* in most editions. The attention is on the beauty of the

The last five words of the paragraph I named *60910* pose the problem of the viewpoint named futurology in the first, (1), of two senses introduced in the previous chapter. The full possibility and probability pivots on the effectiveness implied by (2) in a full quaint meaning of expressing and of knowledge: "(2) aims at expressing knowledge of history." Expressing then means a lift forward and knowledge means care. Can we move forward to care for history? The last chapter talked of opposing oddities to the new science: a massive global captivity in stupidity and malice and, in the small zone of Lonergan studies, a settled exclusion of Lonergan's view and his optimism.

There is, too, Lonergan's pessimism which still has an optimistic turn. He proposed his view in the context of Christian theology. Would it take? "Is my proposal utopian? It asks merely for creativity, for an interdisciplinary theory that at first will be denounced as absurd, then will be admitted to be true but obvious and insignificant, and perhaps, finally, be regarded as so important that its adversaries will claim that they themselves discovered it."[51]

I have, in various places, written of such disciplines and people as might emerge with the claim of discovering the omnidisciplinary vortex need. Such an operative claim would be a step in the right ethical direction.[52]

---

basket, and explaining radiance, *claritas*, is what "wins the cigar." One could consider that *claritas* adds the aesthetic dimension to Lonergan's notion of thing discussed in chapter 8 of *Insight*. But also there is the matter of cosmic *claritas*, a matter relating to sublating St. Ignatius' final *Exercise, Contemplation for Obtaining Love*, and to futurology's ultimate unity. The aesthetic dimension, vibrant in our what, opens us to the topic of the next two chapters.

[51] The conclusion to his essay, "Healing and Creating in History," *A Third Collection*, edited by Frederick E. Crowe, S.J. (Mahwah, NJ: Paulist Press,1985), 108.

[52] I have referred occasionally to the book by Arjun Appadurai mentioned in note 1 of the Preface, *The Future as Cultural Fact: Essays on the Global Condition*. Now seems an appropriate time to point to a step in the right ethical direction in

CHAPTER 19
THEN WHAT

Again, the paralleling with *Insight* 19 and *Cantower* 19 help here,[5 but yet I still chat, without that richness, to those who climbed with me to see freshly, volley-served, their—your—what-face in the mirror.[54] So now they and you may join me in this bathroom

---

regard to that book, indeed, in regard to the multitude of creative and critical books that are at present surging forth. This book makes my comment easier in that the final chapter, titled "The Future as Cultural Fact," gallantly pushes issues of ethics, possibility, imagination, aspiration, hope. He stands against being stuck in "the lens of pastness." *Ibid*, 285. I can make my own his summary statement of page 294: "By the ethics of possibility, I mean those ways of thinking, feeling, and acting that increase the horizons of hope, that expand the field of the imagination, that produce greater equity in what I have called the capacity to aspire, and that widen the field of informed, creative, and critical citizenship." But what is the right ethical step in regard to this and other books—including my own, and Bernard Lonergan's? It is to flow them into functional research, thus bringing into the ongoing—or really merely seeded!—cycle, both suggesting positive and negative anomalies. Otherwise we "have to be content if their subject is included in a list not of sciences but of academic disciplines." Lonergan, *Method in Theology*, 3. Without that swing into futurology, Appadurai's work, however creative, remains pre-scientific. He is not, of course, going to like me writing that, no more than Branson and company would enjoy reading my comments on their ineffective muddling, nor more than the Lonerganism community is thrilled by my view of their learned devaluation of Lonergan. But the road forward is not a tactic of contrast and comparison of these views: the road is a patient swinging of all this facticity into the cyclic dynamics of the quite new system of futurology.

[53] *Cantower* 19 (available at: http://www.philipmcshane.ca/cantower19.pdf) places the dynamics of the proof of God's existence in *Insight* in parallel with the dynamics of the discovery of the neutrino: an elementary hypothesis generating a fuller hypothesis. The key element to hold to is that by *proof* is meant, not some deductive achievement, but the verification of a hypothesis. One has to give energy to the what-answer to have a serious is-question. In that *Cantower* I spell out in popular fashion Thomas' five ways so as to lift the reflection to plausibility for those reasonably open to it. *Insight*, however, invites the giant climb into a position (*ibid.*, 413) which grounds an altogether more luminous plausibility.

[54] My reference here is to Michael Jackson's song, "Man in the Mirror."

"what then" without the climb through *Insight*'s 18 chapters to the central question of chapter 19, "What, then, is being?"[55]

The full little paragraph there, ending with that question, is worth quoting now to give us the possibility of a radiant context of mirrored *claritas*, radiance.

"The question that leads to the extrapolation has been raised already but not answered. For we have identified the real with being but we have not ventured to say just what being is. What, then, is being?"

In this little book I have underplayed the middle sentence of the paragraph. I have been content to say, in rambling insufficiency, just what **what** is. Your follow-up in radiance to larger radiance is a lifetime ethics of achievement,[56] to be reached by your patiently glowing open vulnerability to the interpersonal relating that is at its best in the astonishments of artistry and understanding and wit and "the tranquility of darkness."[57]

Let us move on then with our chat, inviting round our cranial molecules the wash of the other two sentences. I have, I hope, raised your what and mine in these pages, and pointed to further possibilities of its raising up so that we might sniff the cigar, in

---

[55] *Insight, CWL* 3, 665. You might enlarge your musing here by seeing this as another title to the first section of chapter 4, "Religion," in *Method in Theology*. The title there is "The Question of God." My perspective above pushes for a lift of that section into a fuller existential aesthetic.

[56] The phrase, "ethics of achievement," as far as I remember, is Whitehead's. See Lonergan's *Topics in Education, CWL* 10, 102: "Here, I think, is relevant Whitehead's remark that moral education is impossible without the constant vision of greatness. Moral education communicates that vision in unnoticed ways. The vision gathers the way dusts gathers, not through any massive action but through the continuous addition of particles that remain." For me, some key unnoticed ways are, e.g., audience resonance to television shows that portray stumbling whatters reaching for excellence in cooking, dancing, dressing for the runway.

[57] *Insight, CWL* 3, 642.

guarding the unities met in our daze, unities of the basket, of the basket cases, and even of the basking in the sun of the tadpole of history. Sachmo can sing his way round the basket cases and the brutalities of the 20th century: "What a wonderful world"; but you may find that beyond your dreams and screams.

And that is fair and fine. If you were expecting here some glib chat about something called *god,* then I am to disappoint you. We remain poised together in, over, about, the **what** that, a little later or in a make-up morning moment, may stand at the baseline of a bathroom mirror, cunningly alert for who might blink first out over the net of glassy nerves, two eyes and I-s, watching one unfold.

That **what** that is you, morning eyed or street-tired, may well be deeply off put by the tadpole tale-wagging of contemporary religious communities. I am, let it be said, Catholic, though perhaps it would be better to pick up someone's suggestion of me being "an independent Christian." Pope Francis has been lauded as a refreshing change; still, who could possibly believe in a Vatican God aligned with a gross over-abundance of tribal laws and rituals, with legislated abuse of women, and with crude mythologies regarding the place of sexuality in being.[58] The Israeli establishment's brutal nazi treatment of East Jerusalem and the West Bank does not say much for the God of the Old Testament. And then there is the Afghanistan situation, the Taliban, the Muslim Brotherhood. None of these gods say hello to a decent what.

---

[58] This is an enormously complex issue. Mathew Fox raises it in a popular religious context in chapter 15, "Sacred Sex," of *One River, Many Wells* (New York: Putnam, 2000). He draws attention to Augustine's twist on the topic, as does Bernard Lonergan in the concluding pages of his essay "Finality, Love, Marriage," *Collection* (Toronto: University of Toronto Press, 1988) *CWL* 4, 17-52. The entire drive of Lonergan's essay puts him at odds with the tradition, and that oddness lurks in those pages.

But I certainly do not wish to get into the Christian thing, nor indeed into the thing of any other religious persuasion. Friedrich Heiler[59] talks of areas common to major world religions such as Christianity, Judaism, Islam, Zoroastrian Mazdaism, Hinduism, Buddhism, Taoism, but the talk is not of facts but of norms. The reality of whatting about ultimacy is that **what** whats in circumstances, and the contemporary witnesses to theism, sadly, do not stand apart from Lonergan's condemnation: "such is the monster that has stood forth in our day."[60]

What I am pushing for is precisely a tadpole or seedling perspective on the emergence of whats and the current seeding of the emergence of whats whats, and here we face the seeding of the larger reach of "then what?" even the then-what of religion's dropouts. So, yes, I ramble into my own past's tradition—you surely have such a past to wander into, Proustwise—when I muse over what it was like for James Joyce to step out of Irish Catholicism and what was it like for John the Evangelist to find himself outside the closed door of the Synagogue and what was it like for Christian women of the Early Church to be nudged aside? So John heart-writes his strange story of his friend's talk at the well with the dicey lady, "'Believe me, woman,' Jesus told her, 'the time is coming when you will not be worshipping the Father on this mountain or in Jerusalem.'"[61] And might Joyce have been writing, in the large of Ulysses Wake, the next seven words, "You do not know what you're worshipping"?[62]

"What, then, is being?" "Then What?"

Who is asking, and in what ontic and phylectic state of story?

---

59 Friedrich Heiler, "The History of Religions as a Preparation for the Cooperation of Religions," *The History of Religions*, edited by Mircea Eliade and Joseph Kitagawa (Chicago: University of Chicago Press, 1959), 142-153.

60 *Method in Theology*, 40.

61 John 4:21. I am quoting the William F. Beck translation, *The New Testament in the Language of Today* (Saint Louis, Missouri: Concordia Publishing House, 1963).

62 The first words of John 4:22, in the same translation.

In the First International Lonergan Conference, Florida, U.S., 1970, Lonergan's views were challenged in two particular areas: there were questions about the validity of his moves in chapter 19 of *Insight* and about his pejorative view of myth in *Insight* 17.1. Who were asking? The majority were in a mythic academic world, somehow outside their own whats.[63] Might we now move, cycle, inside?

Back, now and then, to my question about the question, the what whatting about Then and Now.

Lonergan concludes his first paragraph of the section in *Method in Theology* with the statement, "In each case, there arises the question of God."[64] This is true of his cases, but it is not true of each what, battered by myths and logics. What I have noted above is a comeabout[65] repetition of Xenophanes' insight: "Xenophanes had noticed that men made their gods in their own image and remarked that lions, horses, oxen would do likewise were they able to carve or to paint."[66]

What, now, are you to do as either speaker of ultimacy or as searcher for ultimates? As searcher you need to wend your way to finding yourself as a "Notion of Survival," so that you find a poise of searching or a rock of finding. But the minimum of the finding is an identification of your loneliness in daily being. Forty years

---

[63] There is a general failure to detect, in the first section of *Insight* chapter 17, that the analysis of myth reaches out to contemporary mythological thinking and living. At Florida there was a dominant devaluation of the task of self-knowledge that still prevails in Lonergan studies and elsewhere. The book that I drew attention to in note 1 of the Preface, *The Future as Cultural Fact. Essays on the Global Condition*, however rich in reference and illustration, is symbolic of that dominance. There is in that goodly book no suspicion of the giant task of understanding either oneself or economics.

[64] *Method in Theology*, 101.

[65] See notes 32 and 37 above.

[66] *Method in Theology*, 307. It would be worthwhile to brood over the different context in which Lonergan invites us to consider seriously Xenophanes' view: see *ibid.*, 91, 319, 344.

ago I spoke, juvenilely but wisely, of the same search as occupies us here, trying to give the same words a larger tadpole meaning. "Popularly put, you are larger than the Red Square, taller than Manhattan, deeper than galactic space. Not to contemplate that aspirative universe within is much more than a sorry personal loss."[67]

As speaker of ultimacy I have invited you here to the other dynamic of that final chapter of *Wealth of Self and Wealth of Nations: Self-axis of the Great Ascent*: entering the vortex of functional collaboration, and indeed, also in that final chapter, within the mess of economics. The invitation is for you to swing into a culture where the speaking is not the dark tolling of a monk's bell of logic about God, but a Then-talking in "a ruddy gem of changeful light."[68]

---

[67] I quote from the end of the final chapter of the book mentioned immediately in the text. There follows the relevant Epilogue, "Being and Loneliness."

[68] I am recalling Sir Walter Scott's comments after his visit in 1814 to the Bell Tower Lighthouse.

CHAPTER 20
THEM WHAT

It seems appropriate to select, for my zone of comment on chapter 20, Lonergan's final choice of a conclusion to this last chapter of *Insight*. So I start by quoting the end of chapter 20 which adds a nudge by being the third 80-word doctrinal statement of this little book.

"The solution's development in each of us is principally the work of God, who illuminates our intellects to understand what we have not understood and to grasp as unconditioned what we had reputed error, who breaks the bonds of our habitual unwillingness to be utterly genuine in intelligent inquiry and critical reflection by inspiring the hope that reinforces the detached, disinterested, unrestricted desire to know and by infusing the charity, the love, that bestows on intelligence the fullness of life."[69]

First, I take the hope he writes of here as echoing the hope he expressed earlier in the chapter, a hope which I identify with my project, the global advance to the "specialized auxiliary that is ever-ready to offset every interference either with intellect's unrestricted finality or with its essential detachment,"[70] the project that I have named *futurology*.

The quotation above from chapter 20 is also the end of the short section on "The Identification of the Solution," and that title resonates magnificently with my own efforts, from the beginning, to bring you readers to a slim suspicion that the solution is a subtle contemporary identification of **what**. Lonergan begins the section thus: "there remains the problem of identifying the solution that exists,"[71] and I can make that my claim here also. I

---

[69] *Insight, CWL* 3, 751.
[70] *Ibid.*, 747, conclusion.
[71] *Ibid.*, 746.

am writing of the emergence of a Tower Community about which I have been thinking and writing since 1966. This little book is a fresh and final effort sixty years after the writing of *Insight*. It bluntly weaves the specialized auxiliary of functional collaboration, Lonergan's discovery of 1966, into the secularity that was his bent throughout that first great book. Yet here I leap brazenly beyond that secularity, and indeed beyond Lonergan's frustrated Roman efforts, to try to express a meaning he might have developed had he been allowed to live forward more freely into the existentialism of his 1957 lectures, *Phenomenology and Logic*.[72] The bubbling issue there was a larger view of exigence, of the subject, of dread, of the Field.[73]

That bubbling pushed me forward to try to seize what he might have meant by THEM in the decades after, had he been given contemplative and leisured scope.[74] Might I share that bubbling and push here? I have the same problem as I had at the beginning of chapter 16: a problem of helplessness yet also a need to burst forth with a fresh twist on that broad doctrine that concludes *Insight*. Yet the fresh twist is just that: a twist of doctrine and system that belongs in a definite and indeed remote context.[75] "Them what" points to a large communal enterprise that I wish to identify slimly here for the two groups to which I write: the broad

---

[72] Lonergan, *Phenomenology and Logic*, *CWL* 18, edited by Philip McShane (Toronto: University of Toronto Press, 2001).

[73] See the index to *CWL* 18, under *Field*, and also my comment in the Introduction to that index.

[74] On Lonergan's career see Pierrot Lambert and Philip McShane, *Bernard Lonergan: His Life and Leading Ideas* (Vancouver: Axial Publishing, 2010). Lonergan spoke thus of his Latin treatises: "these things are practical chores that you have to do if you're teaching a class of 650 people." "An Interview with Bernard Lonergan," edited by Philip McShane, *A Second Collection*, edited by W.F.J. Ryan and B.J. Tyrrell, Darton Longman and Todd, 1974, 211. In the beginning of *The Ontological and Psychological Constitution of Christ*, *CWL* 7, Lonergan is quite blunt: "it was because of teaching obligations that I was led to write the book and not because I had nothing else to do." *Ibid.*, 3.

[75] On the significance for growth of context, see Lonergan, *Word and Idea in Aquinas* (Toronto: University of Toronto Press, 1997), *CWL* 2, 238.

loose group of those interested in having a role in the globa[l] future; the quite precise small group of those interested in th[e] work of Bernard Lonergan. My first inclination was to plung[e] forward into talk of "Them what" in relation to my very focuse[d] climb of these past four years.[76] But that focus is shockingl[y] remote from the climb so far in my little chat-book about **what**[.] The shocking remoteness relates to the difficult proximat[e] Christian theological contexts of those four years.[77] There was th[e] climb towards a solution of Lonergan's search for a treatise on th[e] mystical body,[78] and that solution was finally expressed in th[e] book *The Road to Religious Reality*. There was the climb beyon[d] Lonergan's expression of Trinitarian theology and that, as on th[e] move in me and us, has been expressed in the final 8 of my 21 *Posthumous* Essays.

Might I say, in dense vague popular terms, what that clim[b] bubbles forth in? "In": now there's a word, the starting word o[f] *Insight*, that places us right in the primary existential gap that ca[n] emerge, does emerge, **in** this read-**in**-g. **The boldfaced print i[s] now familiar, but not perhaps its me-n-in-g**. At best, I write now[,] positioned and poisitioned, to one that shares that poise in psychi[c] skin, the meant print patterns folding round cranial folds an[d] chemicals, leading to a savoring of the solution to the problem o[f] identification of the chemical **what** that reads. But most of m[y] readers are not thus poised: the poise is of the Tower of Able "in a hundred years or so."[79] Still, what I write in this next paragraph, has it not some common meaning?

---

[76] The climb is represented compactly by the 21 *Posthumous* Essays (available at: http://www.philipmcshane.ca/posthumous.html).

[77] My effort in that last *Posthumous* Essays was to lift Lonergan's Latin works on the Trinity into the psychological context of subject-as-subject luminosity.

[78] See *Insight*, 763-4.

[79] The phrase is recurrent in a poem by Patrick Kavanagh which begins "If ever you go to Dublin Town / In a hundred years or so." The phrase is the dominant mood of *Lonergan's Standard Model of Effective Global Inquiry* (this book is available at: http://www.philipmcshane.ca/lonergansmodel.html).

The what that you are or I am is a reach for story, the full story of that what's journeying in the Field. The journey is identifiable as history, but with my what somehow identified with that full story. Can it be that each what is somehow the whole story, and indeed is cauled to haul it all in, a possession, a possessed? "'All we know is somehow with us .... It lurks behind the scenes.'[80] Skin-within are molecules of cos mi c all, cauled, calling. The rill of her mouth can become the thrill, the trill, of a life-time, the word made fresh. Might we inspire and expire with the lungs of history? But the whole story is you and I, with and within global humanity, upsettling Love's Sweet Mystery into a new mouthing, an anastomotic[81] spiral way of birthing better the buds of Mother."[82]

What, fundamentally, is a whole story. It twines forward towards patterning cranial and fringe chemicals into viable identification.

---

[80] The conclusion to chapter 9 of *Insight*.

[81][Note 80 and this note are in the original. See Philip McShane, *Lack in the Beingstalk: A Giants Causeway* (Halifax, NS: Axial Publishing, 2006), 183-184. I include the entire note as relevant to this little book's message.] *Ana-* again, *stomein*, to provide with a mouth. "Using the device of *anastomosis*, Joyce attempts, in the last chapter of his last work, to bridge all the great ontological chasms." Margot Norris, "The Last Chapter of *Finnegans Wake*: Stephen Finds his Mother," *James Joyce Quarterly* 25 (1987), 11-30, at 11. The device layers into the transition to my concluding page of this chapter. Think of the French for *sea* and *mother*, and move to the final page of *Finnegans Wake*.

It seems as well at this center stage to circle the deeper patriarchal issue. Did Stephen find his mother? Joyce sought to write all not right all. He was a fragmented axial man, fragmented like many of the grated women of his time. Ezra Pound took him to task for his detachment from economics. See my *Shaping of the Foundations*, 73, 75, now on the website. The Russians against the Finns was for him another instance of Finnsagainwake. As he end wounded Finnegan he was unsuccessfully failing to find his daughter, eventually letting Jung have a go at the grated Lucia. And is there not perhaps a madly sane symbolism for post-axial life in Lucia's view of the doctor's mandibling: 'To think that such a big fat materialistic Swiss man should try to get hold of my soul." Quoted in William Wiser, *The Twilight Years: Paris in the Thirties* (New York: Carroll and Graf Publishers, 2001), 216.

[82] The conclusion of chapter 2 of McShane *Lack in the Beingstalk*. See note 81.

The problem of identification lurks in those patterns within the scenes of ancestors and descendants. Cosmos and ancestors greet us with namings of an identity of Them that can be as different as a Zulu serpent and an elephant of India. Where will the long tadpole journey lead? "Identification is performance." It is a what-reaching that is ever bent on co-lecting, a together-reading that the "good, always is concrete."[83] Indeed, returning to the twist in reading **what** that has been present from the beginning of the book, "**What** is good, always is concrete."[84] So we may come to this first sentence of the second chapter of *Method* within the invitation of self-reading the first word there in a molecular Field-searching that is an exigent, de-dreaded, cherishing of "the order of the universe ... with that order's dynamic joy and zeal."[85]

But we are reaching here for a new reading of the beginning of *Insight,* "**In** the midst." What is the identification, "The Appropriation of Truth,"[86] lurking in those 800 pages? What is the identification lurking more slimly in my little book? Let me bring you back with me to my searchings of eleven years ago. That searching is in my third ***Cantower***—aptly titled then for us now, "Round One Willing Gathering"—and has its third section hovering round our problem, with the title "Identifications." So it begins—and I should quote as much as might help beginners and elders alike to sniff the fieldedge on the mountain slope, to sniff the we and them, spinning, an **inn** of their lonely what, to sniff the cigar of radiance, to smoke within. Come with me, then, for a page or so of a walk down a memory lane of a neglected appeal of 2002, an appeal that stretched on for over a million words.

---

[83] *Method in Theology,* 17. I am freshening here the first sentence of the chapter on "The Human Good."

[84] The full first sentence of "The Human Good," *Method in Theology,* 27.

[85] *Insight, CWL* 3, 722, concluding words.

[86] *Insight, CWL* 3, 584. The title of section 2.5 of *Insight* chapter 17, the section upon which I am about to add comments of a decade ago.

"'There is the problem of identification ... ability is one thing, and performance is another. Identification is performance.'[87]

Perhaps if I were to sum up the problem of my ***117 Cantowers*** it would be in terms of **identification** as Lonergan discusses it in this particular section of *Insight*. And perhaps, if nothing else, this particular section of this *Cantower* will tempt you to read that section, gather you willing round it, in a fresh scratching ratting reading.

I could well tackle the invitation to read the section as Aquinas tackles a section of Aristotle, ending up with a text much longer than the original. Indeed, there is a book to be written about the topic. What to do? Throw out a few pointers. And it is useful, in so doing, to number the nine paragraphs of the section. That will be the meaning of the bracketed inclusions, e.g., (9.3) means a third of the way down paragraph 9. Add to this a second piece of my strategy: a parallel that I have used regularly is the parallel between the periodic structure that emerged in the 1860s for chemistry and what I call the hodic structure that emerged in the 1960s for culture.[88]

Immediately we have a problem, the problem of identification: an adaptation of our sensibility (1.8) to be met on the level of experience in its broadest sense (5.5). I speak of culture,[89] not of

---

[87] *Insight*, *CWL* 3, 582. I am leaving the notes as they are in the original text.

[88] I spell this out a little in *Process: Introducing Themselves to Young (Christian) Minders* (available at http://www.philipmcshane.ca/process.pdf) around page 94. An examination of the journals of chemistry in the nineteenth century shows a discontinuity in the 1870s; no parallel discontinuity has so far occurred in theology.

[89] I invite you, at some stage, to pull into your reflections here the section "Culture and Reversal" (*Insight*, 7.8.6). I hope that you will find a lift in your reading of such sentences as "There will be a division of labor and a differentiation of function. There will be an adaptation of human intersubjectivity to that division and differentiation." *Ibid*., 263. The new reading is not, of course, Lonergan's. The cosmopolis of the hodic structure was still thirteen years away.

theology. I think back now to my own struggle towards performative identification, beginning in 1969 with musicology and wending its way to geometry in 1999. You must somehow reach out, if only by a pensive ramble through the full journal holdings of a university library.

In ***Cantower I*** I drew attention to Ezra Pound's suggestion of a dominant image,[90] and my image, as you know, sublates Vorticism. But what do I mean by **my**? What would I wish you to mean by you cultivating **your** image? The word *cultivate* refers to a culture, and a serious culture is a culture of bloodstream and bones. **My** image I eccentrically intussuscepted over more than three decades of daily rumination, molecular cud-rumening. The culture of your grandchildren will, I hope, be such as to cut back the need for eccentric solitude: the periodic structure has now a household. So, I appeal to some eccentric daftness in you to home-in, room-in, the key "dynamic images" (9.3) that "possess in the sensitive field the power to issue forth not only in words but also in deeds" (9.4). The "well-formulated became mine" (6.6) and I would wish it to become you—not just become yours—so as "to generate the stresses and strains in knowledge that will lead to" (6.9) the "more adequate account of reality" (6.9) that is the hodic structure of the search for the being of meaning. The vortex, ***Cantower***, imaging allies our sensibility against "settling down like good animals in our palpable environment" (4.5) of the usual nests and lairs of academic denizen. It battles against plane, plain, and clear meanings, with its new imaging of ex-plane-ing and its infinity of towering. It is "an adapted and specialized auxiliary"[91] to the "boxed in" (8.8) humanity of this axial period, pointing to a

---

[90] "Function and History," *Cantower I* (this essay is available at: http://www.philipmcshane.ca/cantower1.pdf). See the text there at notes 24, 38, and 39.

[91] I am recalling a key piece of the thirty-first place in chapter 20 of *Insight*, page 747. I would claim that the pragmatic answer to the search for such an auxiliary is the hodic structure.

twisting, sloping,[92] round and up in a radical new control of meaning: that "new control of human living can be effective only in the measure that it has at its disposal the symbols and signs by which it translates its directives to human sensibility." (9.8)"

I deviated grandly there with a page or so of remembering themes past, but that remembering perhaps puts a fuller twist on the tale of what in this book, weaving it into an appropriation of the truth of our calling towards circumincession? "Them what"? Them is certainly, for all, us all 100 billion so-far humans, tadpoling our tale and tail with no sense of molecules flexing towards frog legs. Might we align our tale to that emergent rhythm?

Before my deviation I was poised to push further towards the Christian meaning of Them, the +3P to the incomplete sum of human persons in the diagram $\mathbf{W}_3$ that haunts this entire work,[93] a + that, for some, may be a +NP – with N anything from 0 to an unknown X. History is there, dynamically there in "joy and zeal."[94] Are my $\mathbf{W}_i$ "symbols and signs by which it translates its directives to human sensibility"?

And what of the signs that identify history for the Christian as the Symphony of Jesus, and that further identify ***Comparison*** as solving Lonergan's problem, in chapter 20 of *Insight*, of locating a treatise on the Mystical Body of Christ? It is located, rightly, at the beating-forwards heart of theology.

And what of the doctrinal leap that merges the first quotation above, from the end of *Insight*, with a transposition of Lonergan's

---

[92] The structure and strategy of sloping is the topic of ***Cantower VIII***, "Slopes" (available at: http://www.philipmcshane.ca/cantower8.pdf).

[93] See notes 9 and 34 above. I give here only the relevant piece of the first line of $\mathbf{W}_3$: "HS f (p_i ; c_j ; b_k ; z_l ; u_m ; r_n) + 3P"." The **+** is the key issue. Lonergan concludes his 26 point identification of the What of God with "in the twenty sixth place God is personal" (*Insight*, 691): so there is NP, with N being at least 1.

[94] *Insight*, *CWL* 3, 722: the final words.

"four-hypothesis"[95] into an inner searching of the radiant intersubjectivity that makes the tension of participated active and passive spirationalities a dynamic of the inner discovery of ontic and phyletic story, a dynamic of **what** speaking effective in history, "Double You Three in me in all, Clasping, Cherishing, Calling, Craving, Christing?"

---

[95] The hypothesis is expressed in English in the thirteen-line paragraph that crosses from page 471 to 473 of Lonergan, *The Triune God: Systematics* (Toronto: University of Toronto Press, 2007), *CWL* 12. It is to be the source of the intimate spirituality hinted at in the concluding lines of the present chapter. The Tower version requires the positioning and the poisitioning described in *Cantower* 9, "Position, Poisition, Protopossession" (this essay is available at: http://www.philipmcshane.ca/cantower9.pdf), but it goes far beyond my rambles there regarding protopossession. My final eight *Posthumous* essays give leads (see: http://www.philipmcshane.ca/posthumous.html).

EPILOGUE

Those familiar with my previous efforts at pointing towards a global and systematic care of the future will have identified the source of my suggested structuring of that care long before I mentioned, in chapter one, the old guy in Toronto who pointed out the eightfold way to me in 1966. Indeed, they may have detected swiftly enough the twists and turns lurking in the table of contents.

This little book has the same structure as Lonergan's *Insight*: Twenty Chapters bracketed by Preface, Introduction, and Epilogue. But then you must add the twists; mainly the weaving of the chapters of *Method in Theology* into the table of contents, and the contents, in peculiar but I hope enlightening ways.

Those not familiar with either my works or Lonergan's need some guidance here in detecting the weaving, even if the guidance bores those familiar with Lonergan's two major works. Let me put together some pointers. First, I turn to the table of contents of *Method*, and note that chapters 5 to 14 are twisted into the table of my book as chapters 4-14. There is an extra chapter in my list, and that is accounted for by (a) my reducing the two history chapters, 8 and 9, in Lonergan's *Method* to one, 7, in mine; (b) spreading my reflections on Dialectic, a single chapter 10 in Lonergan, into the three chapters 8, 9, and 10. Of course, I have not really cut the treatment of history to one chapter if you consider the meaning of my chapter 2 as, well, bringing to the fore my sublation of "history in the style of Burckhardt rather that Ranke."[96] The oddity of spreading Lonergan's treatment of dialectic—indeed, a single page of that treatment—into three chapters, has different sources. First, that single page 250 of *Method* is the genius page of the book, presenting in cruel brevity the subtle task of that specialty's members. But secondly, the strategy keeps nicely

[96] *Method in Theology*, 250.

parallel, numerically, the chapters 11-14 in my little book with the chapters on the same topics in *Method*.

Thirdly, of course—how much of this is accidental?!—it allows me to parallel chapters 14 on with the rest of *Insight*. Further, the chapter headings from then on echo those of *Insight*, but the word *futurology* enters titles to replace both *metaphysics* and *ethics*.

This is a powerfully suggestive shift. By replacing *metaphysics* with *futurology* in *Insight*'s definition of metaphysics I hope to rescue the neglected aspect of implementation in that definition. Also, the entire project of metaphysics is lifted into the context of Lonergan's solution to the problem of Cosmopolis, and the what-question is given its full ethical meaning. This, no doubt, calls for expansion but that is what the little book has been about.

And it is, obviously, a little book. It is written in a popular fashion, reaching beyond normal Lonergan studies. Yet it is written thus in the spirit of Lonergan's secular approach in *Insight*, and so gets his larger discovery into that context. It is a peculiar contribution to answering the question Lonergan posed to me, as he paced in his room in the summer of 1966, about the possible content of chapter 1 of *Method*: "what am I to do? I can't get all of *Insight* into that first chapter."

It does not answer that question, but lifts the central message of *Method*, effective functional collaboration, into the secular drive of *Insight*. Is it a move away from theology? I do not think so: It lifts the system-thinking of Thomas Aquinas's *Queastio* 1 of the *Summa Theologica* into the new cyclic systematics. It leads the human **what** towards theology in a manner that parallels the leading of *Insight*.

I do not wish to complicate this Epilogue by venturing into differences between my focus on **what** here, indeed on **what-to-do**, to the apparent neglect of **ising**. There are deep issues lurking, in my chat, about the notion of value and about the dynamics of *Insight* chapters 11 and 12 that had best be left to later adventurers. But I would emphasize the importance of taking a fresh serious grip on the manner in which Lonergan introduces the transcendentals on page 53 of *Method,* where there is an emphasis on possibilities. What seems centrally important regarding the focus on adventure, the neglect of ising and of the topic of conversion, is the invitation to the conversion within the question: **Do you view humanity as possibly maturing—in some serious way—or just messing along between good and evil, whatever you think they are?**[97]

This question is repeated here from chapter nine and it gives me the opportunity to identify that chapter's dense asking for a personal life-recollection. It is here, indeed, that the reader who is taking futurology seriously is invited to ask whether their life includes—or is to include in future years—a climb paralleling that represented by the first eight chapters of *Insight.*[98] But I would insist that the climb has the new context represented by the previous eight chapters of my little book, and I would note how this neatly winds the reader into Lonergan's life-concern about economics.[99]

---

[97] The question is posed in chapter 9, but it was originally posed in Q/A 32 and Q/A 56 of the series "Moving Lonergan Studies into Functional Talk" (see: http://www.philipmcshane.ca/qa-23.pdf & http://www.philipmcshane.ca/qa-47.pdf).

[98] As I indicated in note 95, the climb is talked of existentially in my Cantower 9, "Position, Poisition, Protopossession." The drive into *Insight* is the topic of *Cantowers* 27-31. The fuller climb is named on page 286-7 of *Method in Theology* as (1)-(9). In my chapter 11 above I add (10) to Lonergan's list, pointing to functional collaboration. My addition of (11) there is simply a convenience: economic science would fall under the first nine brackets, say at (6). I make no serious attempt, in this short book, to even skim through the first seven chapters of *Insight*, but obviously the Tower Person needs to be at home there.

[99] The structure of my little book led me to omit references to Lonergan's work in economics, but mention was made of further direction in the Epilogue. For the beginner, *For a New Political Economy* (Toronto: University of Toronto Press, 1998), *CWL* 21, is a sound start, but the start has to be selective. A very slow working through the first three chapters of the book gives the astonishing context of a paradigm shift. Then one could move directly to chapter 19. That

Chapter 10 here, paralleling chapter 10 of *Insight*, allows the boldfaced question to be brought into full interpersonal contexts of all varieties of judgment. But entering into detail about that is not possible in our chat. Rather that detail and its significance for the millennial climb is a challenge for you and for later readers, and I would ask for your patience and openness in regard to my strange correlating of the two seemingly different chapters 10.

I availed of that strategy of correlating chapters especially in the concluding eight *Posthumous* essays, but it was a regular feature in the *Cantowers*. The advantage for me is that it allows me to indulge in doctrinal brevity. So, the short chapters of this book that run from chapter 14 to this Epilogue can be considered as pushes forward in the context of the same parts of the book *Insight*. I might claim that they give ways of re-reading *Insight*, indeed in a way that turns the community towards "the inception of a far larger work" that is pointed to at the beginning of Lonergan's Epilogue to *Insight*.

As I mentioned in the Preface and Introduction, I intended to leave Lonergan out of the presentation all the way to the Epilogue, but my strategy spontaneously broke down as I launched into chapter 16. I have little idea now how I might have carried through with the silence regarding that old guy in Toronto. But certainly chapters 19 and 20, as they appear now, are quite a different world from anything that held silent on Lonergan. Chapter 19 here adds an existential context both to the stand taken

---

beginning, in chapter 19, is best backed up by my *Economics for Everyone: Das Jus Capital* (Halifax, NS: Axial Publishers, 1998). The latter work details the key illustration of the invention of the plough and also points to Joan Robinson's rejected efforts to shake up establishment economics. On that topic of shake-up there are also Bruce Anderson and Philip McShane, *Beyond Establishment Economics: No Thank You, Mankiw* (Halifax, NS: Axial Press, 2002), and Philip McShane, *Pastkeynes Pastmodern Economics: A Fresh Pragmatism* (Halifax, NS: Axial Press, 2002). A more fundamental broad context is given by Michael Shute, *Lonergan's Discovery of the Science of Economics* (Toronto: University of Toronto Press, 2009).

in *Insight* 19, a stand which he continued to maintain throughout his life, and to the stand invited in present readers. What is invited is a holding to an openness, in these dark axial times, that may well be the openness of a hidden seeded faith.

Chapter 20 twisted and turned in my minding inspired fingers. With a strange inevitable randomness it wound back round to the problem of a communal identification that is a goal of the incarnation. It also wound back round to the need to wind collaboratively forward about my two key efforts of this decade: [1] the successful—but strangely accidental—identification of the solution to Lonergan's problem of locating a treatise on the mystical body;[100] [2] the beginning of a long post-axial climb to bring the Persons of God into a fresh "eo magis unum"[101] of inner interpersonal intimacy in the persons of the Tower of Able, and thus into a commonsense pressure[102] towards replacing myth by mystery on the pilgrim global roads to our Circumincessional Three.

---

100 This was the central message of the little book, *The Road to Religious Reality* (Vancouver, BC: Axial Publishing, 2012), quaintly titled *Method in Theology 101 AD 9011: The Road to Religious Reality*. It invited a fresh reading of the 101 pages in *Method in Theology* on the forward specialties, with the essential freshness given by a reading of the word *Comparison* of page 250 as "an integral perspective on the weaving sequence of understandings—more or less effective in history—of that incomplete reality" the mystical body. Always there is to be a cyclic revisiting and "the revisiting is to lead, so so slowly, to a new front-thesis on the mystical body, that front thesis eventually to be integrated in the sublated genetic systematics of all such theses throughout the ages." (The two quotations here are from pages 34 and 38 of *The Road to Religious Reality*.)

101 "The more it is one"; the title of the third section of chapter five of Lonergan, *Verbum: Word and Idea in Aquinas*, *CWL* 2, 204. See *Summa Theologiae* I, Q. 27, a. 1.

102 The effective pressure was a Cosmopolis problem raised in the first section of *Insight*, chapter 17.